THE PIONEER EDITOR
IN MISSOURI 1808-1860

The Pioneer Editor

In Missouri 1808-1860

by

William H. Lyon

UNIVERSITY OF MISSOURI PRESS

Columbia · Missouri

ACKNOWLEDGMENTS

While the responsibility for any errors or misjudgments in this book must be mine alone, I wish to express my grateful appreciation for the generous assistance of many persons. To Professor Lewis Atherton of the University of Missouri I owe a special debt for inspiration and guidance throughout the whole of this project. The *Pioneer Editor* would have been impossible without his aid and counsel. For valuable suggestions I am grateful to Dean W. Francis English and the late Dean Frank Luther Mott of the University of Missouri. Others may recognize improvements which they have inspired: Mrs. Gloria Swann, who read the entire manuscript, Mrs. Marjorie Driscoll, who was my typist, and the University of Missouri Studies Committee headed by Professor Albert Brent. The Floyd Calvin Shoemaker Fund provided funds for some of the research. The Committee on Research at Arizona State College provided substantial funds which were used for proofreading and typing the manuscript.

Portions of this manuscript have appeared in journals. I am

grateful to the editors of these journals for permission to reprint portions of the following: "Joseph Charless, The Father of Missouri Journalism," *Bulletin of the Missouri Historical Society* (January, 1961), XVII, 133–45; "The First Missouri Editors' Convention," *Mid-America* (October, 1959), XLI, 218-22.

WILLIAM H. LYON

Arizona State College
Flagstaff, Arizona

CONTENTS

IV FARE FOR THE READER

EPILOGUE

THE PIONEER EDITOR
IN MISSOURI 1808-1860

PROLOGUE

AN ALMIGHTY PEOPLE

I

$\mathcal{B}$EFORE THE War of 1812 the future state of Missouri lay slumbering. Frenchmen had established a society along the Mississippi and lower Missouri which Henry Marie Brackenridge characterized as *paisible* (peaceable, calm). He made his apt description after a journey among *les Illinois*, recording it in his famous "Sketches of the Territory of Louisiana." Judges, codes of law, and prisons were little used. Schools were few and taught only reading, writing, and ciphering. The professional and artisan classes did not flourish. Brackenridge found no tailors or shoemakers and only a few mechanics in the French and Spanish settlements; instead, most people were engaged in agriculture. Living under a simple government, they were little accustomed to reasoning on political subjects.[1]

In their economic affairs the French applied European ideas of economic and social organization, setting up villages and adopting the common field system. These early inhabitants raised farm products to feed themselves, perhaps even raised a little wheat and tobacco for export. Trade with the Indians, hunting, and mining also furnished some with livelihoods.² But it was a lackadaisical society, devoid of public spirit, of enterprise and ingenuity, and incapable of supporting a newspaper.

After 1787 Americans from east of the Mississippi began to drift into the region. Some were slaveholders who left the non-slaveholding Northwest Territory; some were attracted by the more liberal land policy of the Spanish regime. Salt, lead, fur, Indian trade attracted a Daniel Boone, a Moses Austin, a Manuel Lisa, as they had attracted a Laclede, a Chouteau, a Renault, and a La Motte before them. In 1810 St. Louis had a population of 1,100, only one-fifth of whom were American,³ although a larger number of them had settled in the outlying country regions. A migration of Americans had begun up the Missouri River to the Boonslick country, but Indian hostility had forced some of them back.

Then, after 1815, came the driving, relentless American pioneers, who revolutionized this passive society. Up the rivers and along the creeks they emigrated, settling along the Mississippi and the Missouri, and in the mining district south and west of St. Louis. The Salt River country and the country farther up the Missouri (including the Platte Purchase) soon began to receive settlers. The first three decades after the War of 1812 were decades of great expansion: 236 per cent, 1810–20, over the previous decade; 110 per cent, 1820–30; 173 per cent, 1830–40. Ninety-five per cent of the population or more was rural.⁴

In the 1820's the prairie lands began to be settled. General Thomas A. Smith established a prairie farm in Saline County in 1826, naming it "Experiment." Sometimes farmers were forced out of bottomlands by flooding rivers and streams, and learned that corn and wheat would grow where trees did not grow.⁵ The northern prairies and the Ozark plateau were finally settled in the decade before the Civil War.

In the first decades, crops were raised for self-support. But Missouri's economy was supplemented by industry other than agriculture. The fur trade, with its center in St. Louis, and the lead industry around Potosi provided a large volume of business. The Santa Fe trade brought silver from New Mexico into the state.

Why did the emigrants come? Why did they come into the river bottoms and onto the prairies, into the mining fields and into the little villages? Many fled failure in the East; others dreamed of riches from new speculations; all sought new opportunity in the West. They would start life anew. They would become "freemen," with all the dignity and promise which the term implies. A mighty prospect was laid out before them; they intended to exploit it. "Yes, sir," said a newspaper editor to a traveler in Jefferson City, "we *air* an almighty *people*." [6]

II

The decade of the 1840's was a period of great change and transition for Missouri. In many ways it was Missouri's most significant decade. The rate of population expansion fell from 173 per cent, 1830–40, to 77 per cent, 1840–50, and continued to decline thereafter. Urban growth, which could not even be measured in the first three decades because no city of 2,500 or more existed before 1840, rose in the decade 1840–50 by 389 per cent. This was the greatest decade of expansion for St. Louis. Still, rural people accounted for 88 per cent of the total.[7]

The character of the population began to change as well. Non-slaveholders on the prairies of the north and in the Ozarks of the south began to account for a greater percentage of the population, and for this reason slaves accounted for a smaller percentage. German immigration added to the diversity of Missouri's population, which already had French, English, Irish, and Negro elements in it.

In this decade, also, agriculture began to produce for export — the "breaking of the home market." Subsistence, no-surplus farming gave way to farming for profit. Machinery was introduced. Cash crops were raised — hemp, tobacco, and even the staples, corn and oats. Livestock, including hogs and cattle (both on the hoof and as pork and beef in barrels) and scientifically bred mules were exported.[8]

Politics became more institutionalized. Personalities gave way to party organization. The political climate of the second generation produced the great Benton fight for control of the Democratic party and saw the rise of the slavery controversy.

A revolution in the transportation system also got under way. Missouri had not quite started on an internal improvements program when the depression of 1837 interrupted progress. By the mid-1840's a great new interest in roads, especially railroads, began. The counties, the state, and the federal government participated in the building program. By 1860 the state was in debt to the railroads more than twenty-three million dollars, twenty-five times the state's annual average income. Though the 1850's were the great era of steamboating, the railroads redirected Missouri's trade relations. No longer was New Orleans its most important port; instead, Cincinnati, Chicago, and Philadelphia laid claim to the state's exports.[9] Telegraph wires also began to be strung across the state in the 1850's.

Sentiment against the bank and the corporation declined. Limitations upon banking had been introduced in Missouri's first constitution. Severe limitations upon both banks and corporations were included in the proposed constitution of 1845, which was rejected by the electorate. Yet a desire to promote manufacturing and the general economic development of the state led to a softening of attitudes toward bank and corporation. The State Bank was created in 1837 and expanded in 1855 and 1857. Incorporation by procedure was adopted in 1849, though not much used. A great increase occurred, however, in the number of special acts of incorporation which were passed.[10]

All of these factors added up to the beginning of the end of the frontier. The decline of the rate of population expansion, the rise of St. Louis, the breaking of the home market, the institutionalizing of politics, the revolution in transportation and communication, and the rise of the corporation signified the coming of a new era for Missouri.

This decade also began to see changes in journalism.[11]

III

There were four agents which fostered the founding of the pioneer journal: the government, which needed to publicize its laws; the politician, who wished to crystallize public opinion; the literate citizenry, who sought information, amusement, and intelligence; and the printer-editor, who had both altruistic and personal motives. Each agent needed the press to effectively participate in society. All four agents seldom, if ever, cooperated as one in establishing a public journal, but a combination of at least two of them was necessary for setting up a pioneer press. It is this last agent, the printer-editor (and his relations with the other three), which is the concern of this study.

The pioneer editor was not the first to come into the western country. John Mason Peck in his *Guide for Emigrants* described three classes of settlers which, like the waves of the ocean, rolled one after the other into the frontier community. After the explorer and trapper came the first class, the real pioneer, who depended on the free gifts of nature, the game and "range," and who also cultivated a "truck patch" and a crop of corn. This group was succeeded by the second class, who purchased lands and established better lines of communication. Then came the third group, the men of capital and enterprise, who concentrated in villages and towns and who gave to frontier life a more elevated existence.[12] The pioneer editor belonged to this third group.

But of this third group, the journalist usually appeared on the scene somewhat later than other professional men. Ministers rode into the wilderness with the first settlers. Brackenridge in his "Sketches of the Territory of Louisiana," which Joseph Charless printed in the columns of his *Missouri Gazette*, noted the number of mechanics and mercantile establishments, academies, and chapels in the towns of St. Louis, Ste. Genevieve, St. Charles, Cape Girardeau, and New Madrid, but only in St. Louis did he find a printing office.[13] It is quite apparent from the advertisements in the early issues of the *Missouri Gazette* that the merchant and the lawyer had preceded Joseph Charless to St. Louis. George Sibley was enchanted by the settlement at Franklin in 1817, where he found merchants, traders, lawyers, physicians, teachers, licensed tavern keepers, mechanics and two or three reputable preachers. But this frontier village on the Missouri River would have to wait two years for the printing press which, Sibley announced, was about to be established.[14]

In order for a newspaper to flourish in an American community, considerable development beyond the earliest frontier stages had to take place. The editor had to consider many factors in his search for a place where he might publish successfully. He needed a sufficient number of subscribers, both town and country; a reasonable amount of advertising support from merchants, doctors, lawyers, artisans, bereft husbands, and the founders of estrays; adequate transportation facilities to move freight — paper, type, ink, and printing presses; and a regular and friendly postal service to provide low postage rates to subscribers and free exchange between editors. Almost as important to the fortunes of the striving editor was public printing, which provided an extra source of income from the local, state, or national government, and job printing, such as handbills and broadsides. Some of the more enterprising editors even printed books and pamphlets. But when editors first arrived on the frontier, all of these sustaining factors did not always exist sufficiently, and consequently the pioneer newspaper business was at best a precarious enterprise.

The history of the pioneer editor in Missouri involves in a larger sense the history of the Mississippi Valley. His story involves more than merely when and where he published his newspapers; his way of life and his role in frontier society is important as well. Many questions regarding his work and his life need to be answered. Under what circumstances were the pioneer papers founded? What were the functions of the editor as he conceived them? What was the role of politics in frontier journalism? What kind of an enterprise was the newspaper press? How well did the newspaper portray frontier society? What were the conditions of journalism as a profession? What was considered news, and how was it gathered? And what can be surmised about the characters and personalities of the pioneer editors? These questions are dealt with in succeeding chapters.

I FOUNDING A NEWSPAPER

CHAPTER 1

BE FRUITFUL, AND MULTIPLY

I

$\mathcal{W}$HEN ISAIAH Thomas published his famous *History of Printing* in 1810, he recorded as the westernmost newspaper in America the *Missouri Gazette*, the first newspaper in the Missouri and Illinois country, printed at St. Louis by Joseph Charless.[1] Charless had been printing the *Gazette* since 1808 in a village hardly populous enough to maintain an infant journal, even if the out-of-town mail subscribers were added. He began with only 170 subscribers, hardly enough support for even the smallest enterprise.[2] Nor were his editorial talents enlisted in the aid of a political party, except to promote the principles of Jefferson, sentiments almost universal in Jefferson's own territory of Louisiana.

What did lead to the establishment of the *Gazette* was Editor Charless' own zeal as a frontier editor, and the benign attitude, even active aid of the territorial government.

For some years before 1808, territorial officials had felt the need for some more efficient means of publicizing the laws than by sending them to Kentucky to be printed and returned the

long distance to St. Louis. Writing to Secretary of State James
Madison in 1805, Governor James Wilkinson asked that the
federal government send a small type font, paper, ink, and a
press to make it possible for the territory to publicize its laws.
At the same time, and without any apparent collusion, Francis
Peniston of the Bairdstown, Kentucky, *Western American*,
planned to publish the *Louisiana Herald*, in St. Louis (at the
rate of three dollars a year, or for a four-dollar attested note at
the end of the year).[3] Neither Wilkinson's request nor Peniston's
plan materialized; the founding of the first press was left to Joseph Charless.

Ever since this Irishman arrived in America he had searched
for a publication site, but he had not succeeded in either Pennsylvania or Kentucky. Just before he came to Missouri he considered reviving the *Indiana Gazette*, the pioneer newspaper of
Vincennes.[4] Instead he established the *Louisville Gazette*.

A few months later Charless negotiated with the governor
of the Missouri territory, Meriwether Lewis, for the establishment of a press in St. Louis. Governor Lewis wanted operations
begun by June, 1808, when the territorial legislature would
meet, and publication of the revised and new laws would be
needed. ". . . I know not of any point in the U States where I
concieve [*sic*] a country paper or printer would meet with more
encouragement than in St. Louis." So saying, he dispatched to
Charless $225 in bank notes and a bill of exchange on the
Bank of the United States, but since the mail failed to carry it
through, the postrider having drowned in the Little Wabash,
Governor Lewis relied on William Clark to complete the trans-
action.[5] Charless finally came to St. Louis to distribute his undated prospectus, and perhaps he would have printed a paper
in June as Governor Lewis desired, except that he fell ill, and in
the latter part of June and early July was dosed with calomel
and castor oil by Dr. Bernard Gaines Farrar, later an arch political enemy.[6]

Throughout his early career the territorial government gave

him economic aid. In his third week of publication, Charless received an advance of five hundred dollars to publish 350 copies of the laws of the territory, one hundred of which were to be in French. Altogether, in a year's time Charless drew from the treasury $1418.75 for the printing of the laws and the general orders of the militia.[7]

Because of this connection, rumors began to fly that the territorial government controlled the policies of the *Gazette*, and Charless indignantly branded such reports as falsehoods, in the issue of January 4, 1809. He asserted that he was not a mouthpiece of faction, but an independent guardian of the rights and liberties of the people. The *Gazette* "like a faithful centinel [*sic*] will ever be ready to sound the alarm." [8]

So dependent was Charless upon the public printing that he neglected at first to include in his diminutive foolscap folio much else but the national and territorial laws and the militia orders. In the first extant issue, July 26, 1808, he had styled himself "Printer to the Territory," which emphasized his concern for the public printing. Little advertising and even little news appeared in the columns of the early *Gazette*, which so aroused some citizens that they complained of and ridiculed his feeble efforts.

Charless pointed out to his critics that he had promised to enlarge the journal as soon as he had finished printing the laws of the territory, and observed that those acquainted with the difficulties and expense of operating a newspaper in a remote western quarter would make due allowances for any deficiencies. Impatient at the jibes of his detractors, he threatened to increase the subscription price if he enlarged the dimensions of the sheet.[9]

Although Charless had the financial aid of an outside source, he never acknowledged it, and would never admit that the money he had accepted had prejudiced his handling of newspaper affairs. To some extent his self-evaluation was accurate, for he was critical of certain influential governmental figures during the War of 1812, General Benjamin Howard and Governor William Clark. He opposed the creation of the Territory of Missouri and its advancement to the second stage of territorial government, and he worked against the election of the territorial delegate, John Scott. Ultimately, he made himself so obnoxious to political leaders that he lost the public printing. At the end of his editorial career, looking back over his years on the *Gazette*, he noted that to be identified with "Old Charless" was tantamount to high treason, so virulent and powerful had become his opposition.[10]

II

The founding of the second pioneer journal in Missouri arose out of the opposition to Charless by local politicians who raised one thousand dollars (according to Charless), and hired Joshua Norvell, a printer-lawyer from Kaskaskia, of "moderate Republican principles," to edit the *Western Journal*. The "military junto," as Charless branded his opponents, had chafed under his criticism of the clumsy handling of the War of 1812 on the frontier. Mortified and outraged at Charless' attacks on the military for excessive drinking, card playing, and black leg (gambling), and for his criticism of the indulgent treatment of Indians by the courts, his opponents called on him with club and sword in the spring of 1814 to bludgeon him into acquiescense. The air was filled with threats and accusations, without, however, reducing Charless to submission, and so the "junto" proceeded to establish its own newspaper.[11]

On March 4, 1815, Norvell called for the return of subscription papers and began shortly to print the *Journal*. The paper did not suceed, however, and by September, 1816, Norvell had gone to Arkansas. It was revived as *The Emigrant and General Advertiser* by Sergeant Hall probably in March, 1817, who later transferred it to Isaac N. Henry and Evarist Maury in August, 1818. Renamed the *St. Louis Enquirer*, the paper continued its opposition to Charless, with Thomas Hart Benton as one of its chief editors.[12]

Charless continually labeled this opposition newspaper as the "tool," or "hireling" press, and assailed it as subservient to the interests of the politicians whose money had bought it. These aristocrats, as he preferred to call them, endeavored to stifle the freedom of the press in a spirit of intolerance.[13]

In an effort to strike back at Charless, a member of the "junto," William C. Carr, complained that Charless omitted information in the *Gazette* about men whom he disliked and that he otherwise colored the news. Carr was irked by Charless' policy of always crying outrage, junto, starvation of the printer, and death to the liberty of the press, when a rival newspaper was mentioned. Charless' sanctimonious attitude in alluding to the money which Carr and his associates had put up to establish a newspaper particularly incensed Carr, who pointed out that a loan had enabled Charless to establish his press in his day.[14]

III

In later times the two presses established in St. Louis continued their opposition under other men and over other issues. Charless and Norvell and Hall, it is true, were Jeffersonian; their differences were largely over local issues, but even in Charless' later days a party alignment was taking shape.

Charless became the conservative. His paper, renamed the *Missouri Republican* shortly after his retirement, and under the nominal editorship of his son Edward, became a Whig organ. Charless himself, as a private citizen, ardently supported John Quincy Adams in the campaigns of the 1820's.

But the "hireling press," the press of Norvell, Hall, and Benton and its many other editors, drifted into the Jacksonian camp. Indeed one of the directors of the newspaper during the 1820's was Duff Green, who became the editor of the Jacksonian organ, the *United States Telegraph* in Washington, D. C., The *St. Louis Enquirer* and its descendants suffered many vicissitudes — suspended publication, frequent reorganization, one unlucky editor after another. Finally in 1835, the *Missouri Argus* emerged, but even it lasted as a party stalwart only six years.

Newspaper expansion in St. Louis did not take place until after 1830, when the number of newspapers tended to increase more rapidly than the reading public. Editors would complain about this, as an editor of the *Missouri Argus* did in 1835 when he observed that although St. Louis already had eight papers, another was to be added, a German language newspaper entitled *The German Western Advertiser*. Yet, as was the custom then, the *Argus* wished the editors, C. Bimpage and B. J. Festen, success.[15]

If the decade of the 1830's was the decade of expansion,[16] the decade of the 1840's was the time of sophistication. The Census of 1850 registered four dailies; another was probably printed in Jefferson City. This was a decline from previous years, but the census also registered an increased number of literary, religious, commercial, agricultural, and foreign language papers. The city was responding to the more sophisticated tastes of its reading public.[17]

These developments — the multiplication and diversification of the press — were signs of modernization. Journalism in St. Louis was maturing. Further innovations, both technological and institutional, were taking place. The *Missouri Republican* installed its first steam-powered press in 1837.[18] Increased capitalization for plants became necessary. Railroad and telegraph lines, which began to be laid in the late 1840's and 1850's, affected news gathering techniques.

But until these forces began to work their influences, Missouri's first city retained touches of the frontier in its journalism.

IV

Outside of St. Louis the country press remained in the pioneer stages much longer, and in fact it so remained in some areas after the Civil War. At first the number of presses did not increase with any great rapidity, but after 1828 the country press, like the St. Louis press, showed a sharp increase.

The third and fourth journals in Missouri were founded almost simultaneously in 1819. The third, founded by Nathaniel Patten, was located at Franklin (Howard County) and was called the *Missouri Intelligencer and Boon's Lick Advertiser*. The fourth, founded by Tubal E. Strange, was located at Jackson (Cape Girardeau County), and was called the *Missouri Herald*. A controversy developed between the two editors over who had published first.

The controversy was important because only one of the editors could have the federal public printing. At the time Congress allowed only three newspapers in each territory to print the laws of the national government. Strange had planned to publish before Patten, but due to the difficulty of transporting materials to the village of Jackson,[19] he succeeded Patten by several months. Yet Strange laid a claim upon the U. S. Treasury first and got the lucrative contract. Patten was indignant, and felt that he had been cheated, but his letters to the Secretary of State changed nothing.[20] He had to proceed without the coveted subsidy.

Neither Franklin nor Jackson became important towns in Missouri history. Franklin soon disappeared into the Missouri River. Patten moved his publishing plant first to Fayette, then to Columbia. His career in Missouri journalism was long and illustrious, if difficult. It was not so with Strange. Jackson never became a very populous village. Nor was Strange's career to last as long as Patten's. After a little more than a year Strange sold the paper to Stephen Remington, who renamed it the *Independent Patriot*. Remington struggled along with several business partners until the paper finally expired in the late 1820's.[21]

V

In 1824 the Postmaster-General, in accordance with postal regulations, listed five Missouri newspapers out of a total of 597 in the United States. Missouri was near the bottom of the list. Only Delaware with four and the Territory of Michigan with one had fewer, while Illinois had the same number.[22] The five

Missouri papers were the two St. Louis sheets, the *Missouri Republican* and the *St. Louis Enquirer*, the *Independent Patriot*, the *Missouri Intelligencer*, and the *Jeffersonian Republican*, which Calvin Gunn established in St. Charles, seat of the legislature, and moved to Jefferson City when that body moved in 1827.[23]

Daniel Hewitt's List of 1828 showed about the same situation as in 1824.[24] He listed six papers, but he mistakenly listed both the *Missouri Gazette* and the *Missouri Republican*, when in fact the *Gazette* had been renamed the *Republican* in 1821. The "One other Paper" which he listed but could not name was probably a short-lived Jacksonian paper of St. Louis, or possibly the *Independent Patriot*, which may have failed by this time. He recorded one new paper, the *Western Monitor* of Fayette, established in 1827 by James H. Birch, assisted by his brother, Weston F. Birch, and serving the cause of Jacksonian politics.

But these lists and enumerations could not signify the failures, the false starts, the vain efforts of printers who issued prospectuses, maybe even issued a number or two, but did not succeed. In point of fact, Calvin Gunn's *Jeffersonian Republican* was not the fifth journal founded in Missouri; his was only the fifth which was issued over a period of years. Already Robert M'Cloud had failed twice in St. Charles with the *Missourian* (1820) and the *Missouri Gazette* (1823), and once in Ste. Genevieve with the *Missouri Sentinel* (1826–27).[25] Failure had also attended the careers of William Orr on the St. Louis *Register* (1821), and again on the St. Louis *Missouri Observer* (1827–28);[26] of Thomas Foley on *The Correspondent and Ste. Genevieve Record* (1821–22);[27] of Charles Keemle on the St. Charles *Missouri Advocate* (1824–25), on the *Missouri Advocate and St. Louis Enquirer* (1825–26), on the *Etoile of Missouri* (only proposed, 1825), and on the *Missouri Herald and St. Louis Public Advertiser* (1826 and perhaps into 1827);[28] of the editors of the *St. Louis Courier* (December, 1828),[29] the Liberty *Missouri Liberator* (proposed, 1827),[30] and the *Western*

Religious Expositor (a monthly which John Trotter proposed in 1829).[31] All of these papers, either proposed or published, were unsuccessful, and this is not to mention the numerous failures and reorganizations, the ups and downs, through which the second St. Louis paper, the *Enquirer*, had passed.[32]

By the election year of 1832 the Missouri press showed signs of a real awakening. The Whig press was represented only by the *Republican* and the *Intelligencer*, but the Democratic press had increased from the two or three of 1828 to perhaps nine in 1832. Some of them had grown by fits and starts, probably one or two lay dormant, and two of them, the *St. Louis Times* and the *St. Louis Beacon*, which held ambivalent opinions about both Jackson and Benton, which greatly vexed the Democrats, failed soon after the election.[33] One of the supposed party stalwarts, the *Western Monitor*, which had shown so much promise for the Democrats and now showed so much perfidy, had to be replaced. Its editor, James H. Birch, who defected from nearly every political platform, gave way to William B. Napton of the Fayette *Boon's Lick Democrat*, who was later to become attorney-general and state supreme court justice.[34]

In 1836 the Missouri press showed just as much instability, but greater diversity of interest and geographical range. Some editors chose to forsake both Democrat and Whig and support Hugh Lawson White, and there was a growing tendency to forsake politics altogether. Charles Keemle's *Commercial Bulletin and Missouri Literary Register* of St. Louis was supposedly non-partisan, and like several of its non-political cousins of this decade, failed.[35] Religious journals were also founded. Elijah P. Lovejoy's *The St. Louis Observer* carried on a running fight with the Catholic *Shepherd of the Hills*;[36] the Mormons had short-lived monthlies at both Independence and Far West;[37] and the Reverend Spencer Clack proposed a bi-monthly *Baptist Journal* at Palmyra.[38]

Journalism was extending farther into the interior— up into the Salt River country where Palmyra and Bowling Green were located, down into the lead mining district of Cape Girardeau and Jackson, as far south as Ste. Genevieve, where at least an effort was still being made, as far west as Liberty where the *Far West* published for a time,[39] and as far south and west as Springfield, where late in the decade the *Ozark Standard* was published.[40]

In this decade, also, the effort was made to establish a labor newspaper. The first newspaper with a labor emphasis was to be a successor of John Steele's Jacksonian *Missouri Free Press*. Proposed as the *Farmer's and Mechanics' Advocate*, it was finally given the name *St. Louis Advocate*. The editors, J. S. Mayfield and J. B. Bowlin (the latter to serve in the national House of Representatives), announced in their prospectus of October, 1833, that they would maintain pure Democratic principles with moderation and firmness. They favored states' rights, internal improvements under state auspices, and opposed the tariff and the United States Bank. They expressed the hope that any prejudice toward the former press — the *Missouri Free Press* — would not be visited upon them. After a year's issue the sheriff made plans to sell it.[41]

Reorganized as the *Missouri Argus* in April and May, 1835, neither its new editor, Abel Rathbone Corbin, nor his successors, Thomas Watson and Son, stressed the class conflict theme to the same degree as William Gilpin, its third editor, who castigated the "American Aristocracy" for plundering the producing classes. Gilpin's tactics brought violence to the *Argus* and the paper soon passed back into the hands of Corbin, who seems, however, to have lost his crusading zeal. The paper soon ceased publication.[42]

In 1840, at a meeting of the journeyman mechanics, a committee was formed of three from each ward in St. Louis to look into the possibility of a newspaper devoted exclusively to the working man's interests, but evidently nothing came of it.[43]

The Census of 1840 gave a good breakdown of the Missouri press. It enumerated forty printing offices, twenty-two of them in St. Louis. But the majority of these twenty-two were book and job printing offices. In out-state Missouri there was a newspaper for every printing office, all of them weeklies. It is astonishing that nearly half the counties that had newspapers had two or more. Marion had three, and Howard, Cooper, Cole, and Clay had two, while Boone, Callaway, Cape Girardeau, Green, Jackson, Pike, and St. Charles had one, at least on the day the census enumerator came around. Seven were published in St. Louis, one fourth of the total of twenty-four weeklies published in Missouri in 1840.[44]

The number of men employed and the capital invested is also given in the census. Those counties having one newspaper estimated their valuation at an average of $1,500, a figure which seems fairly accurate, even though two claimed they were worth around $2,500, which seems excessive, since most country presses were not capitalized at this high figure. (Printers could be boastful.) In all of these establishments, either three or five men were employed.

Counties with two or more papers showed evidences of the competition. In one county, Cole, where the valuable state printing was available, the valuation averaged $4,000, with four employees in each office, but a county like Marion, which boasted more presses than any other country area, employed eleven men in three offices which were valued collectively at $1,700. St. Charles County figures reveal the influence of close proximity to the St. Louis newspapers. Its one newspaper employed one worker, who labored in an establishment worth a paltry $300.[45]

In the 1840's the country press showed a greater rate of expansion than the state as a whole. Or, to put it another way, expansion in St. Louis had slowed down so that in 1850 the number of newspapers had increased by 31 per cent over 1840, compared to 46 per cent for the weekly press, primarily in the country. As peripheral areas in the state opened to settlement, and new communities rose to prominence, the number of weeklies increased more rapidly than the dailies. Indeed, the number of dailies decreased from six in 1840 to five in 1850, and if the 1850 census taker came around on the right day, he found only four of these located in St. Louis, and one in Jefferson City, where the *Jefferson Inquirer* was issuing a daily during the legislative session.[46]

Diversity was the new note of the 1840's. While literary, religious, and miscellaneous journals were not new in 1840, it was not until 1850 that the census taker made a special category for them, and we may presume that most of the seventeen literary and miscellaneous and two religious journals were published in St. Louis. Seven of the periodicals were monthly, and were probably literary or religious.[47]

The census taker in 1850 did not record any neutral or independent papers, though such organs were published from time to time in Missouri. Yet neutralism was not a paying proposition, and perhaps 1850 was one of those years when the neutralists vainly resisted the artifices of politics. Nor did the census taker mention the German press, though there were five German papers in 1844, and one of them, the *Anzeiger des Westens*, began publishing a daily in 1847.[48]

Newspapering in the 1850's had something in common with the 1820's. Both of these decades were times of shifting political alignments. Political confusion was revealed by papers with anti-Benton, pro-Jackson, or anti-Benton Loco-foco labels.[49] The American party, not destined to become a major force in the nation's politics, captured a number of short-lived adherents in the 1850's. Some effort to avoid politics altogether manifested itself in commercial, literary, or, in the 1850's, temperance bulletins. And finally, beginnings were often quickly succeeded by failures as the year 1860 illustrates.

The four-cornered political contest of that year brought out the requisite number of journals in each cause, and indeed, newspapers represented all kinds of political complexion — Breckinridge, Benton, anti-Benton Democrat, Douglas-C. F.

Jackson (really a Breckinridge candidate for governor), Bell and Everett, anti-Buchanan, Free Soil, Republican, Union, National Democrat, or just plain Democrat. Small wonder that a number of editors avoided confusion by seeking independence! But always the rule was followed that in years of political contest the reading public must have more reading matter, although some of the new-found newspapers did not even outlast the election.

Election years, then, were banner years for founding new newspapers, years when editors performed the function of the fourth estate with diligence and determination.

VI

It is almost a truism that the first journals established in a village, even the first two or three, were destined to fail. There is something almost pathetic about the way James H. Middleton, who was not the first to try in Boonville, reorganized and suspended, time and again, to keep the *Boonville Herald* from final bankruptcy.[50] And a town like St. Charles, located so close to a metropolis, suffered one newspaper failure after another.

Another truism is that as soon as one editor thought of establishing in a town, at least one other editor thought of the same thing. Missouri towns, which today support one or no newspapers, in ante-bellum days supported two or more. St. Louis, with a population today more than fifty times that of 1840, had six dailies then, whereas today it has only two. In Marshall, which waited nearly twenty years for its first journal, three newspapers originated in a three-year period, two of them spokesmen for factions of the squabbling American party, and the third a Democratic organ founded for the express purpose of opposing the other two.[51] No sooner had Nathaniel Patten moved his *Intelligencer* to Fayette in 1826, than a rival was set up in the *Western Monitor*. Such multiplicity was due in part to the editor's overweening zeal, but also to the desire of politicians to combat the heresies of the opposition presses.

Politics came to overshadow all other factors in the founding of pioneer presses. A few printer-editors must have established newspapers from time to time with their own means, while friends and subscribers may have urged and solicited editors, perhaps with money, to begin their endeavors in a certain locality. One such printer, whose name was Francis, investigated the prospects for a weekly in Franklin in 1831, for which he would have required no outside capital to purchase materials and press. Having worked as a foreman in the office of the *Missouri Republican*, he had asked his employers, Edward Charless and Nathaniel Paschall, to inquire of prominent persons in the Boonslick area how well a newspaper enterprise might fare. Charless and Paschall were well enough satisfied with Francis' editorial and mechanical abilities, and, continuing a *Republican* tradition as training depot for Missouri journalists, recommended him highly to Thomas J. Boggs and Abiel Leonard.[52] Leonard must have discouraged Francis, for nothing further is known of his prospective newspaper. But an editor proposing to finance the establishment of his own press must have been uncommon.

The more common method was outlined in the *Missouri Gazette* in 1817 when Joseph Charless, displaying remarkable prescience, reprinted an article from an eastern journal which, he declared, described very correctly the way to establish a newspaper subservient to the views of a faction and useful to the designs of a politician. He published the extract in a fit of pique against his arch rivals, the proprietors and backers of the *Emigrant*, and if allowance is made for his overwrought bias, one has a fairly accurate account of how to set up a press for the purposes of politics.

To start a new gazette, the article read, induce a few individuals to advance from five to fifty or even one hundred dollars apiece to purchase materials, and then procure a printer-editor to manage the infant journal. Such a printer-editor could either be a young man with passion and little worldly experience, or an old man glad to take refuge in any employment he can find. He need not be a practical printer; he might be a lawyer without clients or a doctor without patients. In any case he must be obedient to those who furnished the funds to establish the paper.[53]

Charless could not know how prophetic for Missouri journalism these words were. They described the pattern for the establishment of so many presses. Fortunately, we have at hand in the Dunklin Papers information which confirms Charless' thesis on instituting a newspaper.

VII

In 1832 Democrats began to think of a secure and loyal press when the heretofore official organ of the party, the *St. Louis Beacon*, edited by Charles Keemle, forsook pure Jacksonian politics on the Bank and internal improvements issues, and dropped the names of Daniel Dunklin, Lilburn Boggs, and the whole Democratic electoral ticket from its columns. Alarmed at the prospect of a temporizing policy in the forthcoming election, Governor John Miller wrote to Dunklin and suggested that five or six confidential friends each contribute two hundred dollars to set up a new press in St. Louis, or that they buy the press and type located at Ste. Genevieve, belonging to Lewis F. Linn, and establish a paper in Potosi, Dunklin's home town. They could hire a printer from St. Louis to come to Potosi, he suggested, and Henry Shurlds, also a prominent politician of Potosi, could take charge of the editorial department.[54]

To this Dunklin replied that while Linn's press could be had on good terms, and he knew that William Orr, who had edited some papers in St. Louis, desired to publish a paper in Potosi, he did not believe that a journal could succeed in such an anti-Democratic area. However, Dunklin pointed out to Miller that a certain John Steele had contacted him about a press of "orthodox doctrines" which he intended to set up in St. Louis, and if Steele proved to be the sort of editor the times called for, Dunklin would give him all the aid his means permitted.[55]

Alive to the implications of the *Beacon*'s defection, Steele had already written to Dunklin urging Dunklin, the gubernatorial candidate, to grant his proposed newspaper, the *Free Press*, his wholehearted support. In letter after letter, Steele hammered home the perfidy of the *Beacon*, its wavering and unpredictable course, and the absolute necessity for a dependable paper which would faithfully trumpet the cause of true Democracy. The *Beacon*, perhaps alarmed at Steele's maneuvers, reinserted Dunklin's name in its political column, but Steele asked Dunklin's permission to intervene with the *Beacon*, placing his name in the *Free Press* where he would then triumph over the trimmers, eleventh-hour converts, and open opposition.[56]

In April, Dunklin received the first numbers of the *Free Press*. However, since he remained cool to Steele's proposition, the newspaper editor exerted himself at even greater length. He called attention to his own virtues of firmness and perseverance, and to the *Beacon*'s inconsistency and duplicity. He tried to drive a wedge between Dunklin and his two friends, W. H. Ashley and a General Jones, by pointing out that W. H. Ashley, an opponent of the Democrats, now controlled the *Beacon* and that the opposition had considered nominating Jones against Dunklin for governor. Here Dunklin caught Steele up, for he was able to check Steele's assertions, and he refuted to his own satisfaction the charge that Ashley dominated the *Beacon* and that Jones was a clandestine political enemy.

Undaunted, Steele continued to write feverishly, pleading for Dunklin's open endorsement. To demonstrate his financial solvency, he stated that he had paid for all materials, and had no debts, except about twelve hundred dollars in property-secured notes, which he could use to expand his paper. Why should not the party support what his perseverance merited, he asked? Writing late at night, as late as 3:00 A.M. when his expressions showed the effect of fatigue, he assured Dunklin that he could be trusted.[57]

Dunklin was wary of Steele's endeavor. As he explained to him, and also to Governor Miller, the Democratic party in Washington County had already been deceived by promises in the prospectuses of the *St. Louis Times* and the *St. Louis Beacon*; it could not support the *Free Press* until it had some "earnest" of Steele's capacity for right principles and integrity. "This county is sore from pretenders," he lamented, and Steele would have to show himself worthy of patronage. Finally, Dunklin received a rather unfavorable report concerning Steele from St. Louis, and although the state gave Steele some of the public printing, he struggled against such overwhelming odds that the *Free Press* died a slow, painful death.[58]

Though they had failed to support John Steele, the Jackson men still did not have an adequate press, since even the *St. Louis Times* and the *St. Louis Beacon* shortly ceased publication. In 1834–35 the Democrats again began to canvass the possibilities of a press of their own, for they had heard about an opposition newspaper soon to be established in Jefferson City during the current session of the legislature. Believing in the efficacy of the press, they realized that they must set up a newspaper to forestall the opposition, lest the people read its journal and turn against the Democrats.[59]

The Jackson partisans explored a number of possibilities. They attempted to recoup their fortunes in Fayette by giving aid to William B. Napton, who first published the *Boon's Lick Democrat* in December, 1834.[60] They also had a strong St. Louis paper under consideration, the *Missouri Argus*. Jefferson City presented a problem, since Calvin Gunn already published the *Jeffersonian Republican* there, a good Jacksonian paper, but not considered formidable enough to parry the thrusts of the *Salt River Journal*, a Whig organ preparing to move from Bowling Green to Jefferson City for the legislative session. Either Gunn must take in a partner and enlarge his newspaper, or an entirely new press must be established in the capital city.

Gunn kept his own counsel and played a watchful game.

While he never repudiated any overtures to take in an associate, he procrastinated or named a very high price, and a renovation of his paper never took place. Two partners for him were suggested, Alonzo W. Manning of St. Louis and Foster P. Wright of Bowling Green. Without Gunn's explicit approval, Dunklin even asked Manning if he would edit the revitalized newspaper, but Manning refused to leave his own lucrative business to accept. For a brief time Abel Rathbone Corbin edited the *Jeffersonian Republican,* but he soon moved to St. Louis to become the editor of the *Missouri Argus.* The Democrats pressured Gunn by threatening to relieve him of the public printing, which they did, but all efforts to add a partner to Gunn's enterprise failed, and he remained the master of his own press.[61]

Since Gunn failed to cooperate, the Jackson partisans considered establishing a new press in Jefferson City and entered into negotiations with Charles Keemle, whose press and aparatus now lay idle. They even persuaded Keemle to promise to come to Jefferson City to help get them started. Keemle informed them of the necessary items to set up a journal and offered to sell his materials for one thousand dollars, a figure considerably below Gunn's bid, but still too high for the Democratic politicians. While Gunn improved and enlarged his sheet, the principal Democratic organ soon arose in St. Louis. Abel Rathbone Corbin made the *Missouri Argus* a bonafide Democratic paper, and, although Dunklin distrusted him, he forged the paper into a party stalwart.[62]

The Whigs showed somewhat more success in founding newspapers, and, for instance, established the *Boon's Lick Times* in Fayette, in 1840 with Cyrill C. Cady as the editor. Cady came from the office of the *Missouri Republican,* the leading Whig journal in the state, and immediately rushed forth to do battle with the *Boon's Lick Democrat,* the Jackson paper in Fayette. James H. Birch, the renegade Jacksonian editor, arranged the deal for the Whigs. Birch issued a prospectus under the dateline of the Central Committee Rooms of Fayette, in which he stated the vital necessity of a press to the strength of the Whig party in the Missouri River counties.[63]

VIII

Conceived in this climate—the vital necessity of a press to politics—the 1830's were a time of great flowering for the Missouri press, but also a time of many failures. Most failures were the result of a lack of business acumen. But three newspapers came to a violent end, which served as a warning to editors not to be too fearless and truthful.

In 1832 the Mormons established the *Evening and Morning Star* in Independence, 120 miles west of any town in the state with a newspaper at that time. Its editor, William Wine Phelps, devoted most of the journal to religious matters, but in an inadvertent reference to the abolition of slavery he excited the ire of the already seething Gentiles of Jackson County, who disliked the tactless, energetic ways of the Saints and their unorthodox views on the Indian and the Negro. Gathering before the printing office, the mob refused to grant the Mormons time to remove to another location, and destroyed the building and pied the type.[64]

The second Mormon press faced a similar crisis. The editors had issued several numbers in Kirtland, Ohio, before setting up their monthly in Far West in Caldwell County, Missouri, in July, 1838. This time it was the state militia, acting much like the mob in Independence, which ravaged, burned, and even massacred at Haun's Mill, forcing the Saints to bury press and type to be saved for later use at Nauvoo. So ended the fortunes of Latter Day Saint journalism in Missouri.[65]

The third case of an editor victimized by an irate mob occurred in St. Louis, where Elijah P. Lovejoy criticized in his *St. Louis Observer* the roasting alive of two Negroes. A crowd then assembled before his office and destroyed his printing materials. The cynical Harriet Martineau commented that the St. Louis newspapers feared to condemn the outrage on Lovejoy's St. Louis newspaper, and the incident only confirmed her low opinion of the American press. The *Missouri Republican*, however, scored the mob as "lawless banditti," although the *Missouri Argus* was unwilling to go so far. Lovejoy removed his press to Alton, Illinois, and resumed publication there, but again he skirted too close to abolition doctrines, and while defending his press from a vengeance-seeking mob, he was killed.[66]

CHAPTER 2

PROSPECTUS AND PERFORMANCE

I

$\mathcal{T}$HE PIONEER editor did not casually plant his paper in the virgin ground of the frontier. He carefully cultivated the soil on which he hoped his paper would grow and prosper. Before publishing his first issue, he circulated in the community his prospectus — a declaration of his program and principles — which he presented as a presage of future endeavors and an earnest of good intentions. If a person agreed sufficiently with the editor's credo to become a subscriber, he signed the subscription paper which came as a part of the prospectus. Sometimes, when signers to the subscription list failed to come forward in numbers great enough to sustain his labors, the aspiring editor saw his plant wither and die before it bore any fruit.

This prospectus was much like the doctor's or lawyer's shingle, which announced the physician or solicitor open for business; but the editor, never content to publish only one, issued a new prospectus from time to time, when he wished to increase circulation, to enlarge his paper, or to bolster a sagging business. Thus, the editor revealed to the populace the working hypotheses and the principles which would govern the editing of his proposed newspaper — the soil which would succor and nourish the struggling plant to life and fruition.

In many ways, one prospectus was much like another. They were all similar in content, as, for instance, the very first one which Joseph Charless distributed among St. Louisans in the spring of 1808.

> It is self evident that in every country where the rays of the Press is [sic] not clouded by despotic power, that the people have arrived to the highest grade of civilization, there science holds her head erect, and bids her sons to call into action those talents which lie in a good soil, inviting cultivation. The inviolation of the Press is coexistent with the liberties of the people, they live or die together, it is the vestal fire upon the preservation of which, the fate of nations depends; and the most pure hands officiating for the whole community, should be incessantly employed in keeping it alive. It is now proposed to establish a Weekly Newspaper, to be published by subscription at St. Louis, to be called the

MISSOURI GAZETTE
AND LOUISIANA ADVERTISER
By Joseph Charless

Charless then stated that the columns of the *Gazette* would speak for themselves and he need not state his creed, yet not taking this profession seriously, he then set out to enumerate the principles upon which he sought patronage.

> To extinguish party animosities and foster a cordial union among the people on the basis of toleration and equal government; to impress upon the mind that next to love of GOD, the love of our COUNTRY should be paramount in the human breast; to advocate that cause which placed Jefferson at the head of the magistracy, and in fine to infuse and keep alive those principles which the test of experience has so evidently portrayed its merits, to these ends shall the labours of the *Gazette* be directed.

To men of genius Charless issued an invitation to contribute letters and articles to his journal, but he warned them that he would "invariably exclude" every production which defamed or violated the sacred private life of an individual. He promised to include in the *Gazette* a wide range of information:

> No endeavours nor expense shall be spared in procuring the earliest Foreign Intelligence, which shall be impartially given and a particular attention paid to the detail of domestic occurrences, with extracts from the proceeding of the state and national legislature — To diversify scenes, we shall glean whatever may be most instructive and amusing in the Belles Lettres with historical and Poetical extracts.

He concluded his prospectus with a passage in French which promised to the *habitans* of Louisiana three columns in their native tongue every week, a promise never fulfilled, followed by a statement of terms on which subscriptions and advertisements could be bought.[1] So ran one statement of intent and purpose.

II

The pioneer editor, in his various statements of intent and purpose, recognized the heavy responsibilities which rested upon his shoulders as a conductor of a public journal. The first editors had problems to deal with which resulted from their remoteness from the more civilized centers in the East. After transporting press and type to the scene of publication, no mean task, the editor had to see that he was well supplied with paper and ink. Since transportation to the frontier was hazardous and irregular, the best laid plans of the printer often went awry when supplies failed to arrive. The beleaguered editor then had to apologize to his stern and exacting readers for delay in publication or for the use of inferior newsprint.

The newspaper editor's awareness of his responsibilities to society stemmed from his conviction of the vast influence of the press upon society. The press was a school of instruction, a preceptor of right moral principles, and a Truth disseminator. It brought intelligence, freedom, and virtue into full view.

One of the pioneer editors, Calvin Gunn, told his readers in the *Jeffersonian Republican* that the leading distinction between ancient and modern times was the quick and inexpensive diffusion of knowledge through the press.[2] The pioneer journalist conceived of the press as one of the most powerful agents for raising the educational level of society and for dispelling ignorance and superstition. Since the invention of printing, civilization had seen great progress in the arts and sciences, in the decrease of the numbers of the illiterate and the untutored.

Of all the portals to knowledge, periodical journalism opened the easiest and most accessible way. It brought a greater appreciation of the social graces and the fine arts. It brought amusement to the cultivated taste. Editor Thomas Hart Benton thought that newspapers were in America what the forum had been in Greece and Rome, and declared them "'the most powerful levers which can be applied to the human mind.'"[3]

The pioneer editor recognized his responsibilities, not only to lift the dark veil of ignorance and superstition, but also to act as a purveyor of truth and morality. He announced as his aim the inculcation of truth and moral integrity; he chose as his motto "Principles, not men."[4] Nathaniel Patten and Benjamin Holliday adopted the maxim:

> Truth being the first principle of virtue, and with it stands inseparably connected; and virtue being the only sure basis upon which any government can rest, it will be the first object of this newspaper to make truth, on all occasions, its polar star.[5]

Governor Daniel Dunklin urged Charles Keemle, the backsliding editor of the *St. Louis Beacon*, to stand resolutely behind the Democratic party on the theory that the press was a moral, rather than a political-legal, instrument; his steadfastness would "point to it [the newspaper] as the pioneer of public sentiment."[6] In thus importuning Editor Keemle to play an active role in the Jacksonian party, he expressed the conception of the newspaper as a moral agent in pioneer society. The pioneer editor expressed his own belief in the role of the newspaper in maintaining principles by assuring his patrons that he would always remain fearless and tell the plain, unvarnished truth.

In dealing with the problems and responsibilities of conducting a newspaper the editor pledged his best energies to the publication of a well-conducted and a well-printed journal. If error and shortcoming crept into the newspaper, the reader was asked to make candid allowances for such imperfections, for they would not be due to a lack of hard work and thrift. And many editors attributed the hard work and thrift thrust upon them to a stingy and tight-fisted public. The frugality of editors was not so much a virtue as a necessity.

The editor would persevere, yet the reader had a responsibility also. For the editor was dependent upon the liberal patronage of intelligent citizens. By referring to readers as enlightened and enterprising, he hoped to appeal to their vanity and obtain subscribers. All depended on the patronage and punctuality of subscribers. Whether the *Intelligencer* lived or died, said Nathaniel Patten, depended upon the public. The people of nine western counties, where he hoped his paper would circulate, must decide whether or not they would secure the advantages of a free press.[7] Robert M'Cloud and Stephen W. Foreman, who proposed to publish the *Missouri Gazette* in St. Charles, recognized their dependence on the good will and loyal support of the people of Missouri and avowed that if they ever deserted the real and substantial interests of the public, they would expect to be abandoned by it.[8] But the good people of St. Charles failed to respond to the promises of M'Cloud and Foreman, since the proposed newspaper never went to press.

III

In his prospectus the editor laid out the kind of news his journal would contain. His conception of news was very broad, including agricultural, commercial, literary, moral, and religious essays, foreign and domestic intelligence, and the proceedings of Congress and of the territorial or state legislature. He would endeavor to discuss all questions of public interest, including all conceivable types of information and literature.

His news would be broad in scope because he wished to appeal to every group in society. He wanted to make the newspaper an agreeable companion, a "social friend," [9] in every circle. The two essential objects of a newspaper, affirmed James C. Cummins of the *Missouri Gazette*, were amusement and information.[10] On this basis, editors extended an invitation to every group in society, and assured every class, from the preacher and the politician to the merchant and the mechanic, and both sexes that they would always find in the newspaper something for "gratification, information or amusement." [11] Patrons would also find the journal a family newspaper; any man who denied himself and his family the privilege of a good newspaper was guilty of a gross negligence.

But the editor did not assume full responsibility for the elevation of principles and the conveyance of information and amusement. He extended the privilege of discussing timely subjects in his columns to all who cared to express themselves, declared that a due regard for public sentiment would always keep his columns open to the public, and that he would observe a becoming respect for public opinion. Theoretically, he placed few restrictions on communications from the public, except that they must be fair and temperate discussions in a "mild and manly" manner. A few editors, like James Lusk of the *Jefferson Inquirer*, admitted only subjects which the editor had not already pre-empted.[12] Thus public opinion could play an important part in shaping the character of a newspaper; the public recognized that at least a segment of this opinion, Whig or Democratic, influenced the policies of the editor.

Invariably, the pioneer editor extolled the region where he planned to publish. To spread a correct knowledge about his community in order to attract immigration, to make known the advantages of the state, and to encourage its growth and improvement would be the loyal design of the editor who sought subscribers. By observing the great promise of the fertile, growing section, and by noticing the potential wealth and resources of the "magnificent region," the editor would lend a helping hand to develop its greatness and hasten its onward march.[13] He thus proposed to bind his newspaper to the progress of his community.

His patriotism spanned both community and state, extending to the West and to the nation as a whole. When Robert M'Cloud proposed to publish the *Missouri Sentinel* in Ste. Genevieve, he asserted that on all subjects of states rights and domestic policy the *Sentinel* would be a Missourian. The paper's aims would be to develop the rich resources of the mineral district where it was situated. M'Cloud would also defend the rights and claims of the West and support the constitutions of the state and of the United States.[14] Duff Green and P. H. Ford pledged the *St. Louis Enquirer* to a national policy consistent with Washington's "Farewell Address."[15] A predecessor of Green and Ford, Editor Benton, championed the great West — *"it is time that western men had some share in the destinies of this Republic."*[16]

IV

Politics did not escape notice in the prospectus. Although early prospectuses were more restrained in their affirmation of politics, later ones were more blatantly political in tone, due to the increased partisan activities of Whigs and Democrats. Tubal E. Strange, Thomas Hart Benton, and Nathaniel Patten, who began editing papers in 1819, simply announced their politics as Republican and, like Joseph Charless before them, adhered to the principles of Jefferson.[17] Some of the later prospectuses, however, were nothing more than political pieces. The *Metropolitan* of Jefferson City, for instance, was announced as a Democratic paper, and one of its prospectuses, issued eight months

after its first publication, was a straightforward party testa-
ment.[18]

Many of the editors affirmed that their paper would be a
handmaid to no party. But newspapers were to be critics of
public men and measures and were to guard the rights of the
people, and this meant editors could hardly ignore the political
world. A determined effort to stay out of local elections might
be made, but in practice this seemed as futile as attempting
to remain neutral in state or national politics.

Thus while the editor sometimes disavowed any attachment
to political parties, he did not intend to eschew politics. Curtis
P. Anderson and Charles Groll of the *Weekly California News*
(1858) proclaimed as their slogan "Independent in All Things,
Neutral in Nothing," thus posing as free political agents, but
political, nevertheless.[19] As a practical matter, however, the editor could hardly avoid alliance with one political party or another. James C. Cummins of the *Missouri Gazette* disclosed a
desire to be independent in local politics, although he doubted
if he would be given credit if he were. And, resignedly, he admitted he would be as independent as times permitted.[20]

In all political discussions the editor asserted moderation as
the ideal. He promised to exclude all personal abuse and recrimination, but he was unable to fulfill his ideal of moderation. A
more realistic editor admitted he would not be able to speak
impartially as long as there were honest differences of opinion
in political matters. Robert M'Cloud virtually departed from the
theme of moderation when he told the people of Ste. Genevieve
that he would assail "heresy with every weapon of honorable
warfare," but at the same time he had "no disposition to immo-
late the heretic."[21]

V

The prospectus also proclaimed the newspaper as a sentinel
of the public rights. The right of suffrage, the liberty of conscience, the freedom of speech and press, and the separation of
church and state must be guarded with zeal and vigilance. "But

what must be dearer than . . . our boasted freedom," declared Nathaniel Patten, "which is intimately connected with the fate of the press." [22] Without the press, so vital to the founding of our nation, we would now be under the hand of tyranny and oppression, asserted Thomas P. Green and William Johnson of the *Independent Patriot*.[23] And Stephen Remington, first editor of the *Independent Patriot* stated:

> That the general diffusion of political intelligence, is the only sure guarantee of the existence and purity of a republican government, is a fact deduced from history, and confirmed by experience; where that intelligence has been wanting, the decay of this government has ever been certain and inevitable.[24]

Moreover, the newspaper as a public sentinel would not be effective without a wide circulation. Thomas Hart Benton believed that no citizen should run the risk of losing his rights. Education was the first duty of a republican citizen to his children, and public intelligence his first duty to himself. The first came through schools, the second from newspapers.[25] If there ever was a time for taking a newspaper, maintained F. M. Caldwell and Benjamin Charles of the *Boonville Observer*, it was now when so many pertinent issues demanded public consideration.[26]

Doubtless the newspaper would not have thrived had the editor and his patrons not held the concept of freemen. John B. Williams and R. H. Miller declared their adherence to this concept in the first issue of *The* (Liberty) *Weekly Tribune*:

> As citizens, of the proudest and freeest [*sic*] country which date the face of the globe, we have cherished political measures, for the supremacy of which we shall contend, but not as bigoted partizans knowing no toleration, but as American freemen having with all our fellow-citizens a common destiny.[27]

How were the rights of the public to be protected? Principally, by a perusal and scrutiny of the records of public servants and of their measures. "There is no *freeman* but can find time to read a weekly newspaper," declared Nathaniel Patten,[28] who believed it his duty to censure officials when necessary, however disagreeable the task might be, and stated that he would never shrink from this duty from fear of the loss of any officer's patronage.[29]

Thus the prospectus disclosed the framework within which the editor would prepare copy for the printing press. It revealed the editor's concept of his newspaper as a moral agent, a sentinel, a preceptor, a "social friend," and an advertiser of the resources of community and state. Freeman would use the paper to keep abreast of political events, and by communicating their own views would help mould public opinion. At the same time, the editor, devoted as he was to society and to the region where he was situated, would be the keeper of his own conscience, and reserved the right to express his own views on all occasions.[30]

VI

But what of the actual performance of the newspaper? What was its real function in society? The pioneer editor failed to fulfill to the letter the aims stated in his prospectus. Tubal E. Strange was fully aware of this when he told his prospective patrons:

> It has always been a custom amongst new beginners, when about to undertake the arduous task of publishing a *newspaper*, to make many promises and professions which they are seldom able to perform; but the case is very different with the undersigned, who, well aware of his responsibility, intends plainly to assure the public that he will use his best endeavors to publish a useful and beneficial paper to the community, which shall never be made the vehicle of party spirit or personal corruption.[31]

The pioneer editor also failed to record for the historian, the economist, the sociologist, or even the political scientist all the facts which the modern scholar considers significant. He did represent some traits of his society — its political virulence, naive literary tastes, love of the dramatic, belief in the automatic progress of the locale, inability to separate personality from principle, large concern for national and foreign news and de-emphasis on local news. But he did not portray adequately agricultural concerns, the commercial world, religious life, and the ordinary social relationships of the workaday world.

Agricultural information in the newspaper carried on a rivalry with other kinds of news, particularly political. True, the editor frequently admitted that agriculture was fundamental to the economy and resolved to insert essays on the subject, but since he was no farmer, he could contribute nothing original on the subject, and only clipped items from eastern journals and farmers' periodicals. Allen Hammond of the *Boonville Observer*, who wanted to give more space to agriculture, admitted he could not promise much until after the approaching political contest should end.[32] Patten solicited communications from his readers on agricultural experiments which would be interesting, not only to farmers of the Boonslick, but also to his readers along the Atlantic.[33]

Essays which the editors included in their papers treated such diverse topics as the advantages of manuring; how to treat corn to prevent birds from eating it; how to destroy sheep ticks; the value of deep plowing; and the improvement of general crops.[34] The editor advocated the introduction of Merino sheep and hemp growing, two favorite subjects for agricultural improvement. After the labors of Jesse Buel, Luther Skinner, Edmund Ruffin, and other easterners made scientific agriculture popular, Missourians became familiar with their reforms through reprints in their newspapers.[35] In 1848 Missouri had its own agricultural journal, the *Valley Farmer*, which later merged into *Colman's Rural World* in 1856.[36] However, an editor such as William F. Switzler, who used his paper as a vehicle for the promotion of all sorts of schemes, was most ineffectual in his advancement of agriculture.[37] The pioneer editor seemed least at home in the most prevalent of pioneer occupations — agriculture.

As advocates of civic improvements the editors exerted themselves occasionally in behalf of economic and social advancements. They encouraged educational institutions most often, but also gave desultory mention to libraries, more secure jails, better roads, more fire equipment, and charitable endeavors. Early in his career, Editor Patten coupled a notice of a proposed seminary of learning with high praises of the Boonslick country, and trusted that the climate of his region would be salubrious to Genius and Art.[38] The growth-conscious *Missouri Republican*, noting a deficiency of schools in St. Louis, urged that the city provide free schools to encourage immigration, as many other cities of the United States had done.[39]

Editors seldom initiated action in the interest of municipal improvement, but did present pertinent information to bolster the movement. Noting that the citizens of St. Louis had at last aroused themselves to the necessity of organizing fire companies, Joseph Charless published facts and figures on two proposed fire engines; on ladders, hoops, and buckets; on transportation costs from place of purchase to St. Louis; and gave advice on how to organize fire companies.[40] However, the journalists usually followed the line of Joseph Charless' successor, Edward Charless, who merely gave editorial and moral support to such projects as the St. Louis Library Association and the Female Charitable Society,[41] but carried on no crusade in their behalf. During Patten's long editorial career he wrote only four editorials on good roads, a subject of vast importance to pioneer society.[42]

One of the Missouri editors, William F. Switzler, distinguished himself by his active role in initiating civic improvements through his newspaper, the *Missouri Statesman*. As a matter of fact, Switzler had much to do with the piloting of Missouri journalism out of its pioneer period. He was an active proponent of the University of Missouri. His columns contained much agricultural information, and he was a great advocate of the Boone County Fair. He campaigned in behalf of a number of railroads, including the Pacific Railroad and the North Missouri Railroad, and for plank roads and graded roads. He also favored municipal improvements in Columbia, and at one time or another recommended improved streets, a courthouse, a graveyard, hotels, and fire prevention. Very often he met defeat through public apathy, and very often he overestimated the value of some of his programs.

But Switzler had a technique for arousing public action which often brought results. He usually began with a description of the proposed project, giving information on construction, costs, durability, profits, and about other projects of like nature in other parts of the country. He would then issue a call for a public meeting to inaugurate the program. At the same time, he might appeal to special interest groups who would benefit by the proposal, editorializing his own opinion of the method of completing the project, and picturing the glory and riches it would bring the community.[43] Such a technique was too advanced for the average pioneer editor, who as a participant and not a promoter, often did not go beyond moral sanctions.

A researcher in economic history would find the pioneer journals informative about a number of items, among which are accounts of "emigration," descriptions of newly opened town sites, and land-office sales.[44] Only the figures for land-office sales could be considered accurate since they came directly from the United States Land Office. The other subjects were treated by recording impressions, made inaccurate by a desire to extol or sell. Too often, unverified, spectacular news found its way onto the printed page. Editors rarely made a sustained effort to obtain information other than political. When the Santa Fe trade began at Franklin, the *St. Louis Advocate* jostled Nathaniel Patten, the editor in that town, into cognizance of it and criticized him for overlooking the subject in the columns of his *Missouri Intelligencer*.[45]

Other economic information might be found. During depressions correspondents ruminated on remedies for regaining prosperity and discussed measures in a political context, but made only weak analyses of causes and were rarely in agreement. As civilization advanced and the frontier receded, there was an increase in the reporting of Prices Current, especially in the St. Louis newspapers,[46] and of reporting of steamboat landings by newspapers in port cities.[47]

VII

How dependable was the pioneer journal as a mirror of frontier society? Do its columns give an accurate portrayal of Missouri society before the Civil War? To this question the Frenchman Tocqueville gave a qualified yes.

Speaking of the American press in general, Tocqueville characterized the newspaper as a primary sociological and political record, with the periodical the sole dependable record of young America. Impressed with the meager records of public and private life which were committed from generation to generation by oral and traditional methods, he designated newspapers as "the only historical remains in the United States." Indeed, he believed that in fifty years more would be known of the French in the Middle Ages than of the Americans in the age of Jackson.[48]

But on this point, Tocqueville no doubt overstated his case. Records other than newspapers exist from which to reconstruct the social and political conditions of the past, though it cannot be denied that pioneer newspapers are invaluable as social documents. Nevertheless, the frontier newspaper as a mirror of society leaves much to be desired.

So much a part of his society, so immersed in his microcosm, the pioneer editor gave an impressionistic and individualistic view of his world, a view not based on any academic, reasoned, or well-ordered principles. The newspaper was not so much a mirror as a pattern in the mosaic of frontier society. Its faults were society's faults, its virtues society's virtues.

The pioneer editor was simply not a chronicler of his local community. He felt no compulsion to act as a reporter of local events, and since he never endeavored to analyze his society, the historian finds it difficult to make a synthesis from the newspaper files alone. That the pioneer newspaper failed to mirror society is due in part to the pioneer editor's conception of his function. He was less interested in society than in the individual; his concern was not for customs and mores, but for the actions of men. He thought of his newspaper as useful and ornamental, but not analytical. He expressed himself in favor of "right" political principles, and not objectivity. His era had not yet learned of the methodological concepts of a Max Weber. This was not the Age of Analysis.

Fortunately, a perfect example of the usefulness of a newspaper in reconstructing a pioneer society exists in the files of the *Missouri Intelligencer* published from 1819 to 1826 at the now extinct town of Franklin, opposite the present site of Boonville. Since no physical remains of this early Missouri town have survived the encroachments of the Missouri River, our only knowledge of the place is gained from manuscripts, public records, and Nathaniel Patten's newspaper. Of the first two, precious little remains, but of the latter, the complete files are extant. What was the nature of Franklin society as conveyed through the columns of its local newspaper?

This is the question which Jonas Viles attempted to answer in his article in the *Mississippi Valley Historical Review* entitled "Old Franklin: A Frontier Town of the Twenties." His attempt to reconstruct a frontier town, mostly through the files of the *Intelligencer,* leads one to two conclusions: much about the town must be left unsaid, and much of what is said comes from the advertisements and not from the editorial talents of the editor. Viles could not analyze slavery very well, except to

designate the various occupations which were advertised—
domestic service, wood chopping, general farmwork, and
blacksmithing. The first steamboat touched the wharf at Franklin in 1819, but no further record is made of one until 1826.
While Patten recorded the first shipment of tobacco from the
Boonslick in 1824, Viles could learn nothing, really, of the
vicissitudes of the tobacco trade. In the field of religion, no
church building or organized church appears in the record before 1826. As for recreation, there are reports of hunting, horse-
racing, and banquets, and a normal amount of hard drinking
and gambling may be inferred. The intellectual life of the town
is revealed to Viles only in "tantalizing glimpses." When a local
cause célèbre occurred in the town, Patten barely mentioned
it in his columns. Richard Gentry had shot and killed Henry
Carroll in a duel in 1824. Even though a trial was held, little
can be learned of the incident until four years later, when Carroll's friends used the *Intelligencer* to attack Gentry, who was
running for office.[49]

Yet of all of the pioneer journalists, perhaps Patten reflected
longest on the role of editor and the function of a newspaper
in society, and perhaps he became most dissatisfied with the
results of the editorial labors of his day. Although Patten fell
into the same pitfalls as his contemporaries, he could occasionally separate himself from his times and act as a sort of gadfly to
his profession. In the last year of his life, in what might be considered his valedictory, he castigated his fellow editors. In his
critique, he did not escape entirely from the concepts of his
day, yet he suggested reforms which influenced the practices
of his time and foreshadowed a more modern day.

He entitled his article "Editorial Usefulness," and averred
that the editors would be much more useful to the country if
they abandoned private animosities and low, political abuse and
exercised more judgment in the conduct of their public journals.
Patten felt that under existing circumstances, the high and responsible duties of the editorial profession were prostituted by

a lack of originality, too much vulgarity, and too much concern for politics. "More and more attention is devoted to the manufacture of Presidents, and Governors and *their imps*, than to all the important interests of the country."

He covered traditional ground when he designated the duties of the editor: "to enlighten, improve, and ennoble the minds of the people, to elevate public sentiment, and infuse kind and generous feelings into the bosoms of their patrons." But he began to scratch new ground, when he stated, "We think that the press would be much more useful if its conductors would select more of that plain, practical, common sense kind of information that distinguished the writings of Franklin." Agriculture, commerce, navigation, manufactures, mechanic arts, and statistical information ought to receive proper attention. More space might go to information on the resources, capabilities, and peculiarities of the local country, to education, the fine arts, poetry, and the works of "taste and fancy." He detested mercenary editors, who were bought and hired like slaves to promote the purposes of a political faction.

Patten placed his confidence in local, independent presses, which would not fall prey to the excesses of the profession. Editors would no longer be proverbial for falsehood and misrepresentation, he asserted, if they would but reform.[50]

Thus, the pioneer newspaper portrayed only a limited view of frontier society. Its editor had a tendency to dwell on the bizarre and heroic — what could not escape notice. He overlooked the ordinary events of his locale and the hardships of the workaday world. The pioneer journalists were the Homers and not the Hesiods of frontier society.

CHAPTER 3

BY AUTHORITY

I

𝒯HE EARLY editors of the Ohio and Mississippi valleys rarely went into the wilderness without the assurance of the government printing. The first newspapers were located at the seats of the territorial governments, and the succeeding ones were attracted to towns in which the land offices were located. This printing took several forms: the laws and proclamations of the federal government, the laws, proclamations, legislative journals, and militia orders of the territorial and then of the state governments, and, of course, the less rewarding county and village printing, depending upon the size and activity of these lesser governmental units. The federal, territorial, and state governments paid handsomely for the service of public notice, and the first papers were often little more than legal information sheets. This information was gathered together under the heading "By Authority" to demonstrate the official nature of the publication. Printers avidly sought the subsidy, and since so many of them received it, it seems likely that Missouri and other western states would have waited much longer for their first newspapers under an absolute free enterprise system.

Printers sought the subsidy not only for its financial assistance, but also for the kind of news it afforded, news which their readers sought. When Nathaniel Patten failed to receive an appointment as one of the three privileged printers of the territory in 1819, he marshaled a sizeable segment of public opinion to protest.[1] Knowledge of the laws and militia orders, land office and post office notices, and advertisements for troop supply on the frontier, maintained Patten's supporters, were deemed just as essential to the Boonslick area as to the St. Louis and lead mining districts. This was a day when the citizenry took a greater interest in the laws and legislative proceedings; in that early age of simplicity, our republic laid less reliance upon the lawyer and more upon the individual citizen.

"The Republic is a Goose that all feel at liberty to pluck."[2] So ran the plaint of those editors who had little or no plucking to do. It was perhaps remarkable how many editors performed as public printers. The state government divided out the journals of the two houses, the laws, its job work, the supreme court decisions, and other government printing as many ways as it could. Although the *Missouri Argus* self-righteously condemned the other five dailies in St. Louis for the municipal subsidy which they received, it enjoyed a federal subsidy for printing the laws and treaties of the United States, a subsidy which it gave up before the change in administrations in 1841.[3] In doing so the *Argus* faced the inevitable. Although it posed as a voluntary relinquisher of the government printing — President Harrison would simply have to dispense with the invaluable aid of the *Argus!* — it knew that the government printing would be used as a political weapon after Harrison's inauguration.

The government printing was a reward for the political faithful, and the *Argus* was not among the Whig faithful. Politicians fostered many a newspaper in the first place by providing government largess. Perhaps this kind of support outranked all other means of political subvention. Consequently, many editors were political servants; their policy was to promote and to protect the political connection they had formed.

A few exceptions exist to this rule.

Some editors rose above the meanness of politics, even at some personal sacrifice. This is perhaps the one fact which raises Joseph Charless above most of his editorial brethren. He remained doggedly independent, putting a little substance into the much-touted freedom of the press, but of course he lost the government's business and soon retired from the profession.

Still another editor, Nathaniel Patten, was too honest to accept some state printing which was offered him, but his arch-foe, James Birch, took the job and then distinguished the task with endless delays and wretched typography.[4] Patten was finally given the federal printing, but later Secretary of State Van Buren "reformed" him for his support of John Quincy Adams and handed the plum to Birch in 1830.[5] As Patten prepared to retire from journalism in 1835, he bitterly complained that *"bargain, intrigue and management"* governed the disposition of the public printing, and at such plotting he was obviously not adept.[6]

II

The public printing was an important factor in the political and economic destinies of the pioneer editor. It helped to establish and then to sustain many a newspaper. But Patten was right. In the selection of the government printers, there was much bargain, intrigue, and management. Most often factionalism and politics were involved in the process, as the political history of the public printing will show, beginning with Joseph Charless.

Not only did Joseph Charless print the federal laws, the Louisiana and Missouri territorial laws (evidently the journals of territorial legislatures were not at first prepared[7]), but he applied for and received the printing for the Territory of Illinois until Matthew Duncan established the first newspaper at

Kaskaskia in 1814.[8] His political opposition attempted to take the Missouri printing from him during the session of 1814–15 without success, as the short life of their unsubsidized *Western Journal* demonstrates. So relieved was Charless to get the appointment that he could not restrain himself; he advertised to the whole world his thanks, "with a heart flowing with gratitude." [9] But in 1818 he did lose the territorial printing, and the opposition even circulated the rumor that he had lost the federal printing as well.[10] The territorial delegate, John Scott, worked against Charless, and if Secretary of State John Quincy Adams had not protected him, these rumors about Charless would have been true.[11]

As an omen of the opposition he would face under statehood, the printing of the state constitutional convention fell to Isaac N. Henry and Thomas Hart Benton of the *St. Louis Enquirer.* An attempt was made to exclude Charless by privately accepting the bids of Henry and Benton. When Charless got wind of this coup, he handed in proposals to Colonel Duff Green's printing committee anyway, which prompted Green to inquire who had informed *"old Charless."* His unsolicited bid availed him nothing. Henry and Benton were given the job for nearly $1,100. Charless claimed, after the contract was awarded it must be noted, that he could have saved the people of the state almost $1,000.[12]

Duff Green's history as a Missouri editor, marked by his usual tactics of bombast and dissimulation, was but one episode of his stormy and contentious career. As editor of the *St. Louis Enquirer,* he bid for the state printing for the session of 1824-25, promising to move a press to St. Charles where the legislature then met, if that body awarded him the contract. Award him it did, and the Colonel immediately got into trouble. He so greatly underbid Robert M'Cloud for the task, that he probably could not meet expenses. So he spread the print over the page, with wide spaces and deep margins, thus to increase the number of pages for which he could claim recompense.

Is he not plucking the goose? queried the *Republican*. Editor Green took exception to this and other statements of Edward Charless, who replied, "the elder and younger Charless may have *printed* for the public, but they never undertook to *hoax* the public." Although Green adopted his typical tactics of strict denial to a senate investigating committee, he nevertheless reduced the margins, compressed the type, and increased the lines per page, as any casual observer of the journals can see.[13]

III

For the next thirty-five years the state legislature most often handed the public printing to Calvin Gunn or the Lusk family. These printers did not always win it; political manipulations, shifting alignments, or dissatisfaction with their contract occasionally caused them to lose it. The desire to reward as many party editors as possible frequently diminished their task, yet their persistence and availability brought them many rewards from the public treasury.

Gunn began to print for the state in St. Charles, and followed the legislature from that place to Jefferson City. During the legislative sessions he concentrated on the public printing, reducing the content of his *Jeffersonian Republican* to a bare minimum, sometimes even suspending newspaper operations. This lack of news tempted other editors to move in on Gunn, in the hope of capturing some of the public printing from him, and to relieve the state of the "Egyptian darkness" while the General Assembly met. So proposed James H. Middleton, who probably hoped that the state treasury and the subscribers of Jefferson City could give him the support which the people of Boonville had not.[14] But his plans were forestalled by the editors of the *Salt River Journal*, Adam Block Chambers and Oliver Harris of Bowling Green, who later (1837) edited Missouri's foremost newspaper, the *Missouri Republican*. They proposed moving to Jefferson City during the session of 1834–35 to print for the state and confound the Jacksonian party leaders. The

Democrats now expressed great dissatisfaction with Gunn, but for the most part were unable to get him to enlarge his efforts, and though they threatened to take away the public printing unless he became more stalwart in the party cause, he was an intermittent beneficiary of the state subsidy as late as 1845.[15] Nathaniel Patten observed of Gunn in 1835: "When the teats of the *two* Treasuries [the state and federal] are pulled from him, he will be apt to find himself a little wiser — and a little poorer." [16]

As Gunn gave way the Lusk family moved in. More progressive than Gunn, they issued a tri-weekly and then a daily during the legislative session. Yet the *Jefferson Inquirer* was belatedly caught up in the factional struggles of the Missouri Democracy, a struggle between the Benton and Calhoun factions which in the long run it could not survive.

The first sign of trouble came with the establishment in Jefferson City of *The Metropolitan,* an anti-Benton Calhoun paper, on the eve of the legislative session of 1846. Although the Lusks earnestly desired the appointment of public printer, the Democrats of the legislature appointed Hampton L. Boon, which inaugurated a bitter editorial warfare between James Lusk and Boon. Lusk barely won the public printing in 1849 and 1851, but his victory was due to Whig votes, a fact which Boon never let Lusk forget. And Lusk never let his rival forget the many public offices the generous legislature bestowed upon Boon, culminating his attack in "We have characterized the filthy sheet published in this city by parson Boon, as disunion in its character — as being nothing more or less than the organ of the Calhoun faction — and as having adopted and declared allegiance to the disunion doctrines of the late Mr. Calhoun." [17]

The Whigs had not necessarily wanted to support Lusk; they would have preferred to take advantage of the split in the Democracy and designate a public printer of their own. In 1851 James S. Rollins arranged for E. C. Davis to receive the nod. Yet in reality the Whigs had to make a choice between the lesser of two evils — the Bentonite or the anti-Bentonite — which gave Lusk the crucial votes he needed, although Adam Block Chambers of the *Missouri Republican,* already showing disloyalty to the Whig cause, spoke and maneuvered valiantly in caucus for the *Metropolitan.* But then it leaked out that Chambers had sold the publishers of the *Metropolitan* an old press and type and had no hopes of being repaid unless they were elected public printer. Commented James O. Broadhead caustically, Chambers would have "the Whig party . . . stoop from its high position — lick the dust from the feet of their adversaries — cease to denounce their heresies — smother the expression of their honest sentiments — in order that a miserable apology of a Whig editor might get pay for his old breeches!" [18]

Fearful that Lusk would win again in 1853 by the same ruse, the anti-Bentonites refused to allow a public printer to be elected. Could not Governor Sterling Price take advantage of the Law of 1845 and appoint an anti-Bentonite editor after adjournment? So they planned, but their stratagem backfired when Lusk sought information from the state Supreme Court why he should not continue as public printer. The court interpreted the Law of 1845 in Lusk's favor, and he thus had another two-year term. James Lusk could not know how grateful he should be; in 1890 the Supreme Court reversed its decision.[19]

IV

Bargain, intrigue, and management also form a background for the legal and administrative history of the public printing, which can be divided into three periods: (1) from 1808 to 1825; (2) from 1825 to 1845; (3) from 1845 through the Civil War.

During the territorial period and early statehood the governor or secretary of state usually, though not always, contracted for the printing. Printers presented their proposals directly to the first state General Assembly, however, and that body began to play a larger role, stipulating the number of copies to be printed and placing a ceiling on expenditure. The first general printing act was passed in 1822, which incidentally directed the governor to contract for the public printing. It showed a feeble interest in standards, and, more notably, made the secretary of state the superintendent and the administrator of the public printing.[20]

The second period was inaugurated with the Law of 1825, which also made the secretary of state the superintendent of the printing, suggested a more extensive specification system, and, significantly, made the legislature the decision maker in the selection of printers of public documents.[21] This act was a reaction to Duff Green's effort to fleece the state.

Legislative direction of the public printing was never carried out with much efficiency or unity of policy. While the House and Senate attempted to handle the public printing through joint committees and joint resolutions, select committees and tabled motions abounded. The two-house legislature frequently failed to cooperate in letting out contracts; the state never really adopted an effective specification system, and it usually ignored what policies it made; private contractors almost invariably forced inferior work upon the state; the auction system, whereby printers competitively underbid each other, failed to operate well and was eventually abandoned; the legislature jealously guarded its prerogative, and let no administrative unit assume its role; and politics was invariably an enervating influence.

In seeking bids, the legislature simply scrutinized the specifications the printer offered to fulfill, along with the price he proposed. Because the legislators were not knowledgeable about the printer's craft, they sacrificed high standards for low prices. Then the printer would begin to deliver on his contract cheap and shoddy products, causing the legislature to rise up in wrath. Hammond and Cronenbold, the Whig printers, were finally told by a Democrat House that it no longer had any use for them as printers.[22] Many an editor wrote in the appendix of a journal both apology and justification for inaccuracy and blunder. In the 1830's the legislature scattered the printing over the state, but finally realized that this contributed to low standards, and thereafter concentrated the public printing in Jefferson City.

Not knowing enough of specifications, the legislature fumbled for a policy. It faced several alternatives: it wanted to reward the politically faithful; it wanted to accept the lowest bid and save the state money; it did not want an inferior product. All these were practical considerations which interfered with policy-making. Nor did it know exactly how many copies of the journals, laws, or Supreme Court decisions to publish. There are frequent supplementary editions of the journals and laws lacking a uniform pagination, which should cause the student of legislative history to beware. Since the printers undercut each other for the job to the point where they made a deficit rather than a profit, they sought additional appropriations, and the legislature, though it showed reluctance, usually complied with the printer's request by passing a bill of relief.

Until the session of 1830–31 the public documents were published in either St. Charles or Jefferson City where the legislature sat, but then the legislature took an action which it later regretted; it let the contract out abroad, to James Birch of Fayette. Hereafter, whenever the legislature awarded the contract to someone outside the capital, delay, error, and misunderstanding resulted, as it did in the case of Birch. As secretary of the Senate Birch influenced his own selection as public printer; he could not deliver his product for almost a year; he received compensation before he fulfilled his contract; and when he finally sent it to Jefferson City it sank on a steamboat! [23] Resentment against Birch and his incompetent workmanship was so strong that the next General Assembly passed a punitive law against fraudulent printers, a law never enforced, however.[24]

The only reason for allotting the public printing outside Jefferson City was to reward a party paper. Herein lay an essential conflict: between securing the best contract and subsidizing a political organ. The legislature of 1832–33 deadlocked after great turmoil and finally placed the decision in the lap of the Secretary of State.[25] In the next session it continued to squabble, but it avoided the previous anarchy by accepting the bids of Benjamin Lawhead of St. Louis and of William B. Napton of Fayette. The Secretary of State attempted to remedy the problem of distance by appointing a superintendent of printing to look after the work in St. Louis, but, this supervision notwithstanding, Lawhead was investigated by the next legislature.[26]

Dissatisfaction swelled in each legislature, primarily because it could not end this habit of political jobbery. In nearly every session after the Birch fiasco, a minority supported a bill for the election of a public printer, a reform, it was hoped, to end many abuses. The practical printers supported the measure, thinking it would benefit them and not the lawyer-politician-editor.[27] Finally, in the session of 1844-45, a minority of the printing committee rejected the contention of the majority that the lowest bid was necessarily the best bid. The legislature took its cue from the minority and enacted the Law of 1845.[28]

This act provided for the election by the joint vote of the two houses of a public printer who would do all the printing for the state. It also laid down a specification and inspection system, and pegged prices.[29]

After its passage, opposition to the law continued. Governor John Edwards in two annual messages recommended its repeal. He rightly pointed out that the act did not take politics out of public printing. And he might also have said that it would be difficult to achieve quality by statutory fiat — by a minute description of work to be done and by price-fixing. Edwards had reason to object to the law, for the second public printer, Hampton L. Boon, was an anti-Benton man who vilified Edwards in his newspaper. Boon's workmanship was also poor, and Edwards was convinced that it now cost more than when the printing was let out to the lowest bidder. He proposed, under the proper safeguards, that officers of the government make contracts impartially where terms were the most reasonable, a reform that would take many years to achieve. The legislature refused to drop its politically oriented system.[30] Bargain, intrigue, and management still reigned supreme.

II POLITICS

CHAPTER 4

PRINCIPLES, NOT PERSONS

I

$\mathcal{A}$LTHOUGH Thomas Carlyle did not popularize the expression "fourth estate" until 1841,[1] when he incorrectly attributed it to Edmund Burke, American editors had already exercised the functions inherent in that phrase for several generations. For, indeed, it was in the era of Burke that the American newspaper emerged as a constituent element in the body politic. In the seventeenth and eighteenth centuries the clergy had dominated America, but in the Revolutionary period a great awakening of public opinion occurred, which led the politician to ally with the editor to influence the mass mind. Unlike the minister of a local church, with an outlook primarily parochial, the editor acted as a national agent and promoted the unity of political America.[2] His newspaper voiced the aspirations of an articulate and politically inspired public, who sent to the editor political pieces for publication. As a spokesman of one political party or another, the newspaper reflected a large concern for the electoral processes. Its editor fostered the expression of political sentiments as the natural right of freemen.

The pioneer editor conceived of the newspaper as an advocate of "Principles, not persons."[3] To support mere individual men, without any thought of the fundamental truths for which they stood, constituted a grievous political sin. Such a moral concept led the editor to seek purity and to avoid inconsistency. Politics to him was much like a religion; he crusaded for the faith like a Peter the Hermit, condemning the wayward for their apostasy. As one editor put it, he proposed "to do the honest part of the Country an act of justice in clearing them from the taint of all contaminating alliances by upholding in their name a pure political faith."[4] Another editor who contemplated the honor of political office, Weston F. Birch, assured Abiel Leonard that "To be beaten upon principles can be endured," but to compromise was too much for "a man of feeling to risk."[5]

And so the frontier editor labored in the faith, castigating his opponents and exhorting the followers. Though he made professions of moderation, this did not mean impartiality or neutrality, nor did it restrain his devotion to "right" political principles.[6] Thus he thought of his position as right and that of his rival as wrong, and this moral imperative accounted for verbal and physical abuses of his opponent. Most of the non-political papers, which at first disavowed attachment to a party, either fell into the habit of partisanship or failed to flourish in the limbo of neutrality. Curtis P. Anderson said that he did not intend to publish a rabid political paper; at the same time, he would exercise his right to discuss the political questions of the day, and under this dispensation he could hardly avoid the pitfall of partisanship.[7]

No one assumed more the vitality of the press to American politics than the party leaders of the pioneer period, who sought a press to spread their political doctrines and garner support at the polls. If the party did not have a press, it faced extinction. When the *Missouri Advocate and St. Louis Enquirer* expired, Thomas Hart Benton wrote to Amos Kendall in Kentucky and asked him to come to St. Louis and edit a paper "to maintain the ascendancy of the political principles which you espouse."[8] James H. Birch justified the establishment of the *Boon's Lick Times* in Fayette as an indispensable requisite for the success of the Whigs.[9] Governor John Miller desired a Democratic paper in St. Louis which would boldly and fearlessly advocate and defend the principles of the party.[10] James O. Broadhead understood the need for a Whig press in 1851 to crystallize public opinion at a time when centrifugal forces were dividing and splitting the traditional party alignments into factions and splinter groups.[11] As evidence of a newspaper that altered the voting habits of a population, Governor Dunklin cited the *Western Monitor* for detaching Howard County from the Jackson fold in 1834. He proposed to prevent the same thing happening in Cole County, by either strengthening the *Jeffersonian Republican* or by setting up a new press.[12]

II

Originally the *Western Monitor* had been founded as a Jacksonian paper, the first such politically-inspired sheet in Missouri. Democratic party leaders wanted to swing upstate Missouri to the Democratic party and according to the *Missouri Republican*, a coalition of Missouri and Illinois politicians planned the establishment of two Jacksonian presses, one at Fayette, and the other in Vandalia, Illinois, with the intention of making the "people's candidate" acceptable to the "people."[13] The first editor of the Missouri paper, James H. Birch, denied any connection with Illinois politicians, but he could hardly deny his yeoman labors to influence the "people" in behalf of the "people's candidate."[14]

The notice of the new press did not escape the eye of Nathaniel Patten, who one year before had moved his *Intelligencer* to Fayette. The prospect of a rival press devoted to the election of Andrew Jackson filled Patten with forboding; he denied the remark of Stephen W. Foreman, the editor of the *Missouri Advocate*, that Birch would be in the "midst of the Hero's friends." The people had too much intelligence, independence, and virtue, he asserted, to allow outsiders, tainted with anti-slavery notions, to interfere with Missouri politics.[15]

The Jackson men had originally wanted to buy Patten out, and approached him, asking his price. They also considered a partnership with Calvin Gunn of Jefferson City, editor of the *Jeffersonian Republican*. Neither Patten nor Gunn, however, accepted their offers (Patten declared he did not "feel disposed to abandon a good and *just* cause, for the support of a *bad* one") and the *Monitor* was set up, with Birch its editor.[16]

Then followed a famous newspaper war between Birch and Patten. Birch's bludgeoning tactics, however, fell too hard on the small, deaf Patten, who hated politics, and Birch not only turned Howard County into a Jackson camp, but sent Patten scurrying to Columbia within three years. Looking back upon the episode two years later, Patten noted that his profits had always been small, and when he would have accepted pecuniary aid from the conservative politicians, they offered none.[17] Birch's strident and amoral attacks, and the party's financial aid which filled his coffers, gave him an unequal advantage in his contest with Patten.

III

The founding of the *Monitor* and other newspapers came at a time when King Caucus lay dying and American political leaders searched for new methods of nominating candidates for office. Perhaps newspapers could assume this role. Such a situation occurred in Illinois, where the press figured in the selection of candidates in the late 1830's.[18] Yet the convention system rivaled nomination by newspaper, and ultimately outstripped it as a political device.

These alternate methods aroused considerable discussion in the early 1830's in Missouri. Various epistolary friends of Governor Daniel Dunklin, for instance, discussed the merits and demerits of the convention system, while Dunklin, himself, expressed a preference for the expiring caucus. Since the caucus would not live, however, Dunklin ranked the convention above the press system as his choice of nominating procedures.[19]

Despite the fact that Dunklin selected the newspaper as the less desirable method of nomination, he kept in close contact with newspaper editors on the subject of candidates for office. He carried on a correspondence with Abel Rathbone Corbin concerning his possible successor as governor and his own candidacy for a congressional seat. Corbin, for his part, wished to keep in close contact with Democratic leaders in order to maintain for the *Argus* its official standing in the party. Always careful to sound out the party spokesmen, he asserted that he would only announce candidates in the *Argus* after he had gotten in touch with his political friends.[20]

Dunklin showed the greatest solicitude for the press system in the spring of 1831, when his party had not yet the foresight to adopt nominating conventions, and when it seemed the Democratic party was plagued with a plethora of eager, self-appointed candidates. Moreover, to add to his burden of worry, the *St. Louis Beacon* had dropped the names of gubernatorial candidate Dunklin and his fellow Democratic officeseekers from its columns, and Charles Keemle, its editor, had become an uncertain factor in the party. Dunklin urged Keemle to take the lead in proclaiming Democratic nominees to the public. He proposed that the party unit of each county communicate to Keemle its choice for Congress, for publication in the *Beacon*. Dunklin feared defeat unless Keemle adopted a scheme such as he suggested. Keemle eventually broke his silence and began to print the names of the candidates, but his hesitation, stemming partly from the niggardliness of party financial support, damaged his standing in the Democratic hierarchy.[21]

Four years later, Dunklin urged upon Abel Rathbone Corbin, in even stronger language, the role of selecting candidates. Believing the "Federalists," i.e., the opposition Whigs, had out-maneuvered the Democrats by casting disrepute on the caucus and convention systems, Dunklin asserted that the whole matter of designating candidates rested with the press. He did not believe popular nominations feasible, and he branded cabalistic or junto nominations as highly objectionable. He appealed to Corbin to seek agreement with other Democratic editors in the state, before the *Argus* committed itself. If the *Missouri Argus*, the *Boon's Lick Democrat* of Fayette, the *Jeffersonian Republican* of Jefferson City, the *Missouri Courier* at Palmyra, and the new paper about to be established at Cape Girardeau (probably the *Southern Advocate and State Journal*) all united on two candidates for Congress, the Democratic party would stand a better chance of winning the election.[22]

But as a nominator, the press lacked the essential unity necessary to play an effective role in choosing candidates. Under the circumstances, Dunklin's proposal that five volatile editors agree on two candidates had no chance of success. If the press gained the privilege of nomination, the vainglorious, independent editors would present so many candidates to the electorate that factionalism and discord would replace party unity.

An example of this factionalism was the proposal by the *Western Monitor* that Howard County select its own candidate for governor in 1831. As Governor John Miller pointed out, it would be the very antithesis of unity if every county newspaper followed this procedure.[23] The lack of uniformity and the uncertainty inherent in the press system of nomination was revealed in the case of George C. Sibley, who asked Adam B. Chambers to announce Sibley's candidacy for the United States House of Representatives in the *Missouri Republican*. Chambers demurred, and replied that he would place Sibley's name in the newspaper after he heard from the Central Committee in Fayette. If the Central Committee nominated a candidate, and Chambers expected to learn of this in the columns of the

Boon's Lick Times, he thought Sibley might wish to reconsider his decision to run for political office.[24]

IV

The assumption by the pioneer press of the nominating function was difficult because the pioneer editor often deserted political orthodoxy to follow a course independent of the politicians. Altogether, the editor found it a great strain to be both independent and orthodox at the same time, and in the conflict he sometimes chose his own course as opposed to party policy. In 1841 Abel Rathbone Corbin, so long a steadfast Benton man, finally turned against Old Bullion to advocate soft money doctrines. Benton objected to Corbin's heretical opinions and wrote to Governor Thomas Reynolds that Corbin should somehow be replaced. In October, 1841, Shadrach Penn, a Jacksonian editor of Louisville, bought the *Argus* and employed V. P. Van Antwerp as editor. He renamed the paper the *Missouri Reporter.* But, within a year, Penn attacked Benton as a dictator. Benton then appealed to Governor Reynolds for a loan to Van Antwerp to establish the *Missourian,* which would maintain the principles of hard money. Accordingly, Van Antwerp issued the first number of the new paper in late November, 1843. In 1846, after Penn's death, the two papers, the *Missourian* and the *Reporter,* combined into the *St. Louis Union,* under which a rather testy unity prevailed between the hards and the softs.[25]

The editor whose inconsistency most plagued the Democratic politicians, however, was James H. Birch. During his political and editorial career Birch ran the gamut, from Clay and Adams, to Jackson, to White, to Harrison, to Tyler, and then to Polk. In the early 1830's he had also supported Calhoun, and after his flirtation with the Whigs in the late 1830's and early 1840's, he returned to the Democratic fold, to declare in 1851 that all Whigs were abolitionists. In the Civil War he proclaimed himself pro-union, but it is small wonder that neither Confederates nor Unionists took him at his word.[26]

While editor of the *Western Monitor* and during the period of his combat with Nathaniel Patten, Birch apparently remained devoted to Jacksonian principles, but even in that time he accepted a loan of two hundred dollars from the Clay-Adams party.[27] And soon after Patten left the editorial field to him alone, which was about the time of Calhoun's break with the Administration, Birch showed signs of defection. When he announced himself as a candidate for Congress in 1831, the Democrats expressed great disapproval, for they had already settled on Spencer Pettis as the nominee.[28] Failing to receive the party's nod, Birch now worked actively against the Democrats, so that in 1834 Dunklin branded him a lunatic and later expressed satisfaction that he had quit the party.[29] In 1836 the *Missouri Argus* listed a number of his inconsistencies, castigating him as friend and traducer of David Barton, as enemy and eulogist of Henry Clay, as Democrat in theory and a barefaced European aristocrat in practice, and as both enemy and friend of the banks.[30] Birch epitomized the undependability of the Missouri pioneer editor to the politician, who penalized him for this untrustworthiness by establishing new and rival presses, and by accepting the convention system of nomination.

V

How well did the Missouri press correlate with the political alignments of the state? Any such calculations of the relative strengths of the partisan press is complicated by an imponderable — the circulation figures of the various newspapers, which are largely unknown. Thus, a newspaper of wide circulation, such as the *Missouri Republican*, might be worth two less widely read Democratic sheets.

Certainly before 1832 the number of newspapers in no way presaged the outcome of the electoral processes. Jackson's landslide in 1828 came as a real surprise to the *Missouri Republican* and the *Missouri Intelligencer*, the two Adams papers. The *Republican* found the military hero's victory so repugnant that it wished Jackson had never fought at New Orleans, or that he had lost.[31]

For some reason, the Jackson press seemed in worse straits in 1828 than in 1824. Only the *Western Monitor* at Fayette and the *Jeffersonian Republican* supported the westerner for the presidency, while in St. Louis the Jackson newspapers foundered. The long-standing *Missouri Advocate and St. Louis Enquirer* failed on the eve of election, and the *St. Louis Courier*, which appeared in December after Jackson's election, disappeared after two or three issues.[32]

From 1832 to 1844 the Missouri press generally reflected the party alignments on the Missouri political scene. With the increase in either Whig or Democratic strength, the number of presses of either was likely to increase as well. Yet one may hazard the conclusion that the press was not as responsive to the political situation as it might have been. In 1836 three Missouri newspapers—the *Western Monitor*, the St. Louis *Daily Evening Herald*, the Liberty *Far West*—supported Hugh Lawson White instead of Van Buren, but there is little evidence that they influenced any voters or represented any sizeable group of the voting public.

Probably, in the period from statehood to Civil War, the Whig press showed more signs of stability than the Democratic. The Democrats could boast of no papers with such long, continuous, and influential service under a uniformly consistent leadership as the *Missouri Gazette-Missouri Republican* and the *Missouri Intelligencer-The Columbia Patriot-Missouri Statesman*.

Perhaps, the Whigs had more money than the Democrats to support their press. At least, the *Missouri Argus* thought that the Clay men better supported the Whig country press, as well as that party's city paper, the *Republican*. The *Argus* also believed that the more substantial professional classes bestowed upon the *Republican* the most lucrative advertisements and job work, giving it a financial advantage over its poorer rivals.[33]

Gunn's *Jeffersonian Republican* and the Lusks' *Jefferson Inquirer* had the longest records of any of the Democratic sheets. Gunn began publication in St. Charles in 1824, and moved to Jefferson City in 1827, but his journal did not become an important Democratic paper until around 1832. It ceased publication sometime in the mid 1840's. Under the direction of the Lusks, the *Jefferson Inquirer* stood resolutely behind Thomas Hart Benton from 1840 until its demise on the eve of the Civil War. In St. Louis the *Missouri Argus*, which apparently ranked as one of the most consistent of the Democratic city papers, existed for six years under four different editor-proprietors, who, however, maintained a steady course until 1841. Then the Democrats terminated its career because it had strayed from orthodoxy and adopted soft money doctrines.

During presidential election years in the 1840's, in addition to their regular papers, editors issued small political sheets which came off the press regularly until after the November balloting. In 1840 Ramsey and Paschall published the *Log Cabin Hero*, and J. T. Quesenberry of the *Boon's Lick Democrat*, the *Hickory Club*. Among the political sheets in 1844 were the Boonville *Coon Hunter*, the St. Louis *Mill Boy*, and *The* (St. Louis) *Missourian-Extra*, and in 1848 *The* (St. Louis) *Squatter*. Subscriptions to these political sheets cost around fifty cents.[34]

VI

Though the pioneer editor failed to replace the caucus, or the convention system of nomination, he nevertheless played an important and indispensable role in public affairs. His participation in the hustings and the administration of government was not to be denied him. He took his role in the formulation of public policy seriously. He insisted upon liberty of the press, sometimes turning this liberty into license, and sometimes turning license into the liberty of the cudgel.

CHAPTER 5

THE LIBERTY OF THE CUDGEL?

ℭONCEIVING OF his role in society as a guardian of liberty, a censor of public men and acts, a purveyor of truth, and a medium of public expression, the pioneer editor rarely restrained his ardor. As he sometimes expressed himself with great vehemence, the wonder is that he did not get into more street fights and court suits than he did. He took seriously the advice of Benjamin Franklin in 1789:

> My proposal then is, to leave the liberty of the Press untouched, to be exercised in its full extent, force and vigour, but to permit the *liberty of the Cudgel* to go with it, *pari passu.*[1]

This advice proved too strong for Franklin, however, and he later denounced unrestrained liberty of the press and urged young printers to keep libelous and slanderous material out of newspaper columns.[2]

I

The pioneer editor flourished in a period when reaction to the Sedition Act had reached its apogee, and when the doctrines enunciated by Alexander Hamilton in the Croswell case had received general acceptance. Hamilton had stated in 1803 the doctrine that the press had the right to publish the truth, no matter what the consequences, provided it was done in good faith. He thus denounced the older judicial maxim, the greater the truth the greater the libel.

By the time the first Missouri Constitution was framed, these new-found sanctions for freedom of expression had received general approbation. The bill of rights in the Constitution of 1820 guaranteed freedom of communication and stipulated that in all prosecutions for libel the truth should be admitted in evidence and that the jury should determine the law and facts under the direction of the court.

In the course of time the Missouri legislature placed two restraints on the pioneer editor: he must be wary of charges of fornication and adultery; and he must not incite any Negro to rebellion.[3] While this prohibition on slave agitation scarcely harmonized with the state bill of rights, the Missouri courts would probably have upheld it. The state placed no other caveats upon newspaper expression, and no libel laws as such appeared upon the statute books. Since many editors and their correspondents plumbed the depths of acrimony and abuse, chaotic conditions prevailed on the nature and limits of defamatory statements. A need existed, therefore, for an accurate and workable definition of libel, preferably through a statute. The Missouri legislature, however, did not pass any such statutes until after the Civil War.

The only hope for responsibility lay with the editor. He frequently excluded communications of a slanderous nature. Joseph Charless informed "Petreius" that he could not publish his letter, without knowing his real name, and then only in a paid handbill, for he could never encourage "bush fighting." He also announced to "A Lover of Justice" that he did not wish to encounter a libel, and hence would not print his list of grievances.[4]

II

However, both the pioneer editor and his contributors wrote libelous and defamatory matter for the newspaper columns. When Congress failed to renew the charter of the first Bank of the United States, Joseph Charless triumphantly exclaimed, *"this aristocratic b——d is strangled."*[5] In 1820 he allowed one of his correspondents, "An Admirer of Modern Times," to question the morality of certain of his political opponents by asking "Have they not their housekeepers, and their little ones also? Are they not *philosophically married,* that is to say, wedded to lewdness, revels, routs, &c., &c., &c?"[6] During the struggle for supremacy in Howard County between Nathaniel Patten and James Birch, Birch called John Wilson, who handled Patten's editorial affairs at the time, *"a base calumniator, a dastard and a liar."*[7]

One of the most vehement of all the pioneer editors was William Gilpin, who edited the *Missouri Argus* for its proprietor, Andrew Jackson Davis. Gilpin's editorial career on the *Argus* lasted for only a year. He had branded his opponents as "Federalists," "toadies," and members of the "dung hill breed," and even after Davis received protests against his editor for the use of these epithets, Gilpin continued to assault the fortress of his opponents with "jackass," "poltroon," and "of the vagrant set." This was such strong and vitriolic language that W. P. Darnes, holding Davis rather than Gilpin responsible, beat proprietor Davis over the head with an iron cane. Despite surgery, Davis died, and the newspapers fell back into the hands of its old proprietor, Abel Rathbone Corbin, who kept Gilpin on until after the November elections of 1840.[8]

III

The pioneer editor occasionally ran afoul of the judiciary, which in the first twenty years of Missouri journalism still clung to the remnants of its magisterial prerogative. Clashes with the courts proceeded largely from editorial censure of judicial decisions. Libel as such was not involved.

When the special court of Oyer and Terminer acquitted three Indians of the murder of a white man, Joseph Charless, who rabidly hated Indians, criticized the court in his *Gazette*. The court thereupon cited him for contempt, and forced him to appear before it to declare his respect for the laws and courts of the nation.[9] Presumably, the court considered him purged of the contempt and released him.

Under very similar circumstances, the circuit court haled Charless before it in September, 1820, for an account he had published of his street fight with Isaac N. Henry, a co-editor with Thomas Hart Benton of the *St. Louis Enquirer*. Charless had published his article, stating the facts in such a way as to justify himself and condemn Henry. Charless also instituted suit against Henry for the assault; Henry pleaded guilty, and eventually the court fined him. On the same day that the court fined Henry, his colleague, Thomas Hart Benton, swore out an affidavit against Charless charging that his publication had appeared after the criminal prosecution had begun against Henry, and that in some respects the article contained falsehoods. Benton implied that Charless had attempted to influence the court before its decision had been made. Charless was called before the court to show cause why it should not fine him for contempt, and when he failed to show cause, the court assessed him twenty dollars and costs. Furthermore, the court stipulated that he could not go free until he had paid his fine. Consequently, he languished in jail for some time.[10]

Indignant at his treatment, Charless presented a memorial to the Missouri House of Representatives, praying for the passage of a law on the subject of contempts, to clarify the jurisdiction of the courts in the matter of freedom of publication. Neither the House nor the Senate, however, concurred in Charless' viewpoint, and the House Judiciary Committee reported his petition unfavorably.[11] In these first decades of the nineteenth century, newspapers had not yet achieved the right to discuss court proceedings without judicial reprisal.

IV

Shortly after the Charless case, two others of a like nature occurred before the same circuit court of the County of St. Louis. Patrick H. Ford, successor to Henry and Benton on the *Enquirer,* answered for an article in his newspaper which, it was charged, misrepresented the facts and questioned the motives of the court. The court discharged him after he purged himself under interrogation.

Later in the same newspaper, Luke E. Lawless, a prominent lawyer, published an article complaining of a decision of the circuit court, which had been appealed, although he did not know this at the time of publication. The court took up the matter and decided the article had besmirched its reputation. When the printers purged themselves, the judge filed a second complaint against Lawless. Explaining to the judge that he had unwittingly published the article before conclusion of the case — it was being appealed — Lawless was excused.[12]

He figured prominently in another contempt case, in which he locked horns with Judge James H. Peck of the United States District Court. Lawless had argued a case for the Soulard heirs before Judge Peck, and upon an adverse decision had printed a critical article under the signature of "A Citizen" in the *Missouri Advocate and St. Louis Enquirer.* This irritated the imperious Peck. He summoned Stephen W. Foreman, an editor of the *Enquirer,* before him. Foreman did not intend to bear the brunt of Peck's rage, so Lawless revealed himself as the writer of the piece. Peck then cited Lawless for false and malicious statements and for bringing odium upon the court, sentenced him to imprisonment for twenty-four hours (he got out on a writ of habeas corpus in a few hours), and suspended him from practicing law in the District Court for eighteen months.[13]

Lawless now forwarded a petition to the United States House

of Representatives complaining that Judge Peck usurped powers the laws of the land had not given him, and that he had done so in a cruel and vindictive manner. Four years later, in May, 1830, Congress finally impeached Judge Peck. Much of the argument between Peck's counsel and the managers for the House revolved around the legal question of whether Peck had the right to take Lawless into custody for contempt and pronounce sentence and inflict punishment, without the benefit of a jury. Peck went even beyond the infamous Sedition Act, asserted George McDuffie, which at least provided for jury trial. Both Lawless' defenders and Peck's managers were concerned with the truth, the intent, and the tendency of Lawless' statements against the Judge. And so both sides debated the truth of the Lawless article, and rejected the old maxim, the greater the truth the greater the libel. Where Judge Peck was not modern was in his use of the summary process to inflict punishment for an article in contempt.[14]

Much of the trial centered around the point of law, but the issue of liberty of the press inevitably entered the discussion. Lawless and George McDuffie, his manager, accused the Judge of invading the liberty of the press. Counsel for Peck replied that the Judge had struck, not at liberty, but at licentiousness in the press. Could the press vilify the tribunals and bring them into contempt by gross and wanton misrepresentations? The Judge contended that respectful discussion of the Soulard case, in the public prints or elsewhere, could not take place until after all parties to the suit had laid all pertinent information before the courts, and this applied even while the superior courts heard the case. In other words, newspaper discussion of court proceedings could only follow after the courts had completely disposed and irrevocably decided a question.[15]

Voting 22 to 21, not two-thirds, the Senate acquitted Judge Peck, but the real victory belonged to Lawless, for Congress soon passed a bill which eliminated summary punishments for contempt in the federal courts, except for such cases as outright misbehavior.[16] At least on the federal level, therefore, the sanctity of the courts fell before the liberty of the press, and editors could now enter upon their labors with one further restraint removed.

Lawless participated as a libelant in one more court case, over a publication in a newspaper. This time the roles were reversed: Lawless was the judge, and the *Missouri Republican,* an old proponent of Judge Peck, was the offending party. The *Republican* printed a communication in March, 1836, signed "Witness," which attacked Judge Lawless. Lawless thought at first of refuting the "libel" in the rival *Missouri Argus,* but decided to let the *Republican* prove its charges in a court of law. Unlike Peck, however, he did not hale Edward Charless and Nathaniel Paschall into his court and fine them for contempt. Instead, a bill of indictment was entered in the nearby Lincoln County Circuit Court at Troy. Now the *Republican* cried out "muzzle the press," while the Jacksonian press used the arguments of Judge Peck, once anathema to them, in which they distinguished between the liberty and licentiousness of the press and deprecated these "ignoble attacks upon a public officer." The *Republican,* having just cleared itself of a libel suit in 1835,[17] seemed undaunted by the action of Judge Lawless, and continued its attacks upon him, even though he now filled a federal judgeship as had Judge Peck.[18]

V

The State of Missouri meddled little with the freedom of expression in the press, and when it did, not always with good results. Amidst considerable tumult, the state Senate expelled W. F. Birch as a reporter for some remarks of his in the *Western Monitor* of December 23, 1834.[19] Eight years later the House considered a resolution to summon William Lusk before it for his criticisms of the General Assembly, but the senior editor of the *Jefferson Inquirer* likened the House resolution to the ancient persecutions under John Adams' Sedition Act, and styled it a gag law and a stab at the freedom of the press. The House indefinitely postponed its resolution.[20]

The state actually figured in only one case against a newspaper, the *Lexington Journal*. The *Journal*, under its editor, H. B. Branch, apparently made some unkind remarks about James H. Birch, then a state Supreme Court judge. Judge Birch, who later won a libel suit against Thomas Hart Benton, determined to punish the *Journal* for its "infamous and fiendish" libels, and a grand jury found a true bill in *The State* v. *H. B. Branch*. In 1854 the jury decided that Branch had maligned Birch's reputation, but that he had based his charges on good authority. In such an anomalous position, the jurors hesitated to pronounce sentence, but the circuit judge insisted that they must either find Branch guilty or not guilty, so they rendered a verdict against the editor and fined him only one cent.[21]

VI

About a year before the Soulard case erupted in the St. Louis press, another *cause célèbre* had its beginnings, culminating in a libel suit by one editor against another. Two communications had appeared in the *Missouri Republican* of October 24, 1825, one signed "Q in the Cornfield," and the other "A Citizen of Missouri." "Q" attacked Thomas Hart Benton, while "Citizen" arraigned gubernatorial candidate John Miller. Both articles contained libelous matter, should Benton and Miller so construe it, and this alone would have caused public discussion. But both also made reference to the Thornhill affair, an episode in which Stephen W. Foreman allegedly passed a forged note in St. Charles with Reuben Thornhill's name signed to it. "Q" and "Citizen" had brought Foreman into their animadversions because he had become co-editor, with Charles Keemle, of the Benton paper in St. Louis, the *Missouri Advocate and St. Louis Enquirer*.[22]

Foreman and Keemle demanded identification of the two authors, and Edward Charless delivered up the names Isaac

McGirk and David Barton to the editors of the *Advocate*. The revelation occasioned considerable controversy among the various pioneer editors. Foreman "began to blow out his boiler, and cast his filth," as it was put in the *Republican*, and Nathaniel Patten, although a Clay-Adams man like Edward Charless, disapproved of Barton's slander and devoted nearly two pages of the *Missouri Intelligencer* to testimony in behalf of Miller. The undaunted *Republican* suggested to Keemle that he look into the Thornhill affair and Foreman's honesty, but Keemle stoutly defended his fellow editor for the moment.[23]

However, the business relationship between Keemle and Foreman failed to function well, and the partnership dissolved, amidst charge and countercharge.[24] In the course of time, Keemle became editor of the *St. Louis Beacon* and Foreman of the *St. Louis Times*, and the editorial duel between them reached a climax in a fifteen thousand dollar libel suit against Keemle for defamation of character.[25] However, the court awarded Foreman only five thousand dollars. Although Foreman dabbled in politics from time to time, both his editorial and political work came to an abrupt end in Missouri when he became involved with a ring of counterfeiters. Fleeing southward, he was captured by a posse in Tennessee and brought back to the St. Charles jail. In the denouement, he escaped from jail, to end forever his career in Missouri.[26]

VII

The only newspaper libel suit which reached the state Supreme Court involved Keemle and Joseph Field of the St. Louis *Daily Reveille*, who publicly berated Richard F. Sass, a steamboat captain, for withholding New Orleans papers from them. The editors attacked him both as a businessman and as an employer, by advising his patrons and employees thereafter to ignore him. Sass, "this impertinent person," "this small individual," sued the editors in the St. Louis Court of Common Pleas, and the defendants appealed the case to the Supreme Court, where they lost the verdict. The similarity between this case and the *Cooper* v. *Greely* case in New York was not lost upon the court, nor were they deaf to the counter-arguments of licentiousness. Judge John F. Ryland reiterated the old argument of Judge Peck and his counsel: "The freedom and liberty of the public press will be always promoted and maintained by restraining its licentiousness — *ut vivas, igitur, vigila*" (by remaining ever watchful).[27] Thus the high court warned the editors to avoid malice in their newspapers, lest it bring ridicule and degradation upon those they discussed.

VIII

On at least two occasions U. S. military courts reprimanded Missouri editors. In the election of 1817 for delegate to Congress, a recruiting party, aided and abetted by a sympathetic, carousing mob, stood before the polls, and according to Joseph Charless, brandished knives — even stabbed some people — and intimidated the electors to favor John Scott. Then at midnight they came to the editor's house to play music and throw stones. His account in the *Missouri Gazette*, headed "Military Election," achieved fame far and near and raised a storm as far away as Washington, D. C., where Acting Secretary of War George Graham ordered the commanding officer in St. Louis to hold a court of inquiry. Charless refused to appear before the court, which denounced the article as unfounded in fact and devoid of truth.[28]

The victor in the election, Delegate John Scott, retaliated by refusing to send his congressional newsletter to the *Gazette*, which he labeled a pernicious and barbarous force in the Territory. This accusation hurt, for Charless had declared that one of his primary reasons for establishing a newspaper in the West was to raise the level of civilization. Amidst loud protestations of innocence, he denied the charge of barbarism.[29]

Alphonso Wetmore, an erstwhile editor and at the time a paymaster in the U. S. Army, published in the St. Louis *Free*

Press of August 23, 1832, an article entitled "Molinero to his Paisanos," in which he made some damaging statements about his fellow paymaster, Thomas Wright. He charged him with political subservience to William H. Ashley, a Representative in Congress. The Adjutant-General's Office in Washington, D. C., instituted a court of inquiry to examine the conduct of the two paymasters. The court of inquiry exonerated Wright and found Wetmore's conduct reprehensible and his article based on unjustifiable rumor.[30]

IX

Since all editors indulged in abusive language, they preferred to settle their differences out of court. As long as the pot was calling the kettle black, there was little justification for an editor to go into court seeking redress. When James H. Birch verbally assassinated a number of his political opponents, John Wilson of the *Missouri Intelligencer* leaped to their defense. In his strictures he divulged a misdemeanor case in which Birch was involved while a resident of Kentucky. Wilson's disclosure at first disturbed Birch, but he avoided a court contest.

Instead, he began his rebuttal with a letter: was Wilson impeaching his private character, he asked. Even if he was, Wilson replied, he would not deny the story of Birch's misdemeanor, unless Birch withdrew remarks of his own. The lines were now drawn. Birch did what any good pioneer editor would do; he unloosed a volley of vituperation upon Wilson. Rather than have Wilson haled into court, he set up a private committee of three men to examine the insinuations of the *Intelligencer*. Their acquittal of Birch satisfied Wilson not at all; he merely took four columns to excoriate the committee.[31]

But finally, all other means of settling differences failing, the editor resorted to Franklin's curb on the liberty of the press, the cudgel. Nearly every editor had to meet the prospect of physical violence at one time or another. In the post office at St. Louis, William C. Carr approached Joseph Charless with a pistol and spit in his face. When Charless retaliated with stones, Carr retreated and avoided open combat.[32] At another time a bullet narrowly missed Charless as he walked in his garden.[33] His street fight with Isaac N. Henry has already been mentioned.[34] Other editors also got into fights. James H. Birch waylaid and assaulted Nathaniel Patten.[35] John H. Watson of the *Missouri Argus* attacked Adam B. Chambers of the *Missouri Republican* with a cane.[36] Present, also, at this affair was Thornton Grimsley who perhaps instigated the brutal caning of Andrew Jackson Davis.[37] An aggrieved citizen drew a dirk on James Lusk, but accidentally dropped it before he stabbed him. When W. H. Lusk came upon the scene and saw his brother in danger, he drew a pistol and shot wide of his mark, wounding a thirteen-year-old boy in the hip.[38] William F. Switzler of the *Misssouri Statesman* engaged in fisticuffs with the editor of the rival *Dollar Missouri Journal*.[39] And one editor, J. T. Quesenberry of the *Glasgow Pilot*, suffered a knife wound from an offended correspondent whose communication he had refused.[40]

Thus the pioneer editor, ardent in spirit, devout in the cause, battled for the success of his political principles. Occasionally he carried the struggle into the street, and sometimes he was forced to appear in court. With a religious zeal, he undertook the defense of his party credo. The *Missouri Argus* sent out the clarion call to all the faithful: "Once more to the breach! Once more to the breach, then good friends, and the day's our own." [41]

III BUSINESS AND PROFESSIONAL AFFAIRS

CHAPTER 6

PAYING THE PRINTER

*A*LMOST A year after Charless began his labors in St. Louis, Matthew Lyon, an old printer himself, wrote to a western businessman from his post in Washington, D. C., that frontier newspapers were poor investments:

> There is nothing to be made by printing a newspaper in the country . . . more than half the printers who set up in the Country fail of Getting a liveing [*sic*] by the trade & either go about something else or become journeymen in the Cities. . . .[1]

His comment contained much truth. While patrons were eager to take a paper, they were not so eager to pay the printer, who watched his list of unpaid subscriptions swell until drastic measures had to be taken. Of course, some editors made a success of their endeavors, and others did neither very well nor very badly. But many were complete failures, who fled from one office to another, or retired to another kind of occupation.

I

The ink was hardly dry on his first issue, before Joseph Charless discovered delinquent subscribers, for whose benefit he printed "The Printer's Soliloquy":

> [Our subscribers] cannot think
> That we alone, who publish to the world
> News from all nations, and delight to spread
> Useful instruction through our spacious land,
> Can, meanwhile, live on air.[2]

In entreaty after entreaty he urged subscribers in arrears to pay their debts. For almost two years after starting his paper, Charless reminded his delinquent subscribers that he was made of flesh and blood.[3] To Pierre Chouteau he wrote, in July, 1810, that he possessed more than twelve hundred dollars in overdue bills, which he could collect only at great expense in time and trouble. At the moment, said he, such assets would not help him pay for two arpens of land which he wished to purchase from Chouteau. In this extremity, he offered to pay for the land in a series of installments, or to exchange a field of oats for it.[4] Two years later, Charless was little better off; patrons who had taken the paper for three or four years still owed him more than one thousand dollars.[5]

The pioneer editor thought most earnestly about delinquent subscribers when his creditors were pressing him. At a time of great personal need the editor appealed frantically for money, with perhaps a deadline for when it must be had. Or he thought about his delinquent accounts at the end of the publishing year, when he reflected on the past year's achievements and failures and was preparing to begin a new volume. He dunned his subscribers on these anniversary dates of publication, when it seemed incumbent to show some improvement through the purchase of new materials, and also of course, when old subscriptions fell due and new ones needed to be procured.[6]

When a subscriber did not pay, he should, of course, have been dropped from the rolls. But this easy and simple solution seldom suited the editor. As a matter of fact, he adhered to a policy exactly the opposite: no subscription would be discontinued until all arrearages were paid. The editor hoped to obtain payment by threatening to build up a staggering debt against the subscriber, thus forcing him to pay before he got in any deeper. Furthermore, said the editor, failure to give notice at the expiration of the subscription year would automatically be considered a renewal of the subscription. By saying nothing, the subscriber said "yes." So, while the subscription list remained large, the printer kept on *"working for glory and printing on trust."* [7]

The credit system was the bane of all editors. While Joseph Charless in two years had twelve hundred dollars on his books, Charles Keemle accumulated three thousand dollars in unpaid subscriptions during his first three years as editor of the *St. Louis Beacon*, and he had little hope of collecting even a small percentage.[8] In 1858 the *Jefferson Inquirer* had five hundred subscribers in arrears, one-fourth of its readers.[9] When the *Liberty Weekly Tribune* suspended for a time, R. H. Miller found that he had outstanding two hundred dollars more than the capital invested in his enterprise.[10] The pioneer editor was lenient to a fault in the cautious treatment of his subscribers. He failed to whittle down his subscription rolls because he was willing to extend credit. The rigors of newspaper competition and the lack of coin seemed to require it.

II

One reason for unpaid subscriptions was the scarcity of money in the community. The editor frequently accepted produce — flour, pork, vegetables — in lieu of American specie. Joseph Charless received from John Long two and one-half bushels of corn meal and five dollars in cash, which he calculated quite nicely at six dollars and 56.74 cents. He also accepted, strangely enough, old copper and brass at the rate of one bit per pound, including stills, kettles, and other worn-out articles. Beside the hard-to-find American specie, the printer might also accept "Spanish pictures" (pieces of eight) and notes on specified banks.[11] Money, however, was the great desideratum. As R. H. Miller put the matter: "WANTED, at this office, corn, wood and MONEY. Don't all bring money thro' mistake!"[12]

Ultimately, no matter how cautious the editor was in pruning his subscription list, he had to take drastic measures. Requiring *all* subscribers to pay in advance was too drastic, but some did demand this of all readers residing outside the county or city.[13]

To obtain money from his country subscribers, the editor tried unusual methods. Joseph Charless expected his debtors to send money by members of the territorial legislature, as they came from the interior to assemble in St. Louis. Disappointed in results, he announced he would strike every delinquent owing for two years or more from his lists and place their accounts in the hands of magistrates for collection. This, he assured the laggards, was no joke. He would live up to his intentions this time.[14] Thomas Watson and Son, the new Jasons of the *Missouri Argus*, asked subscribers living in remote places to remit money through legislators, as one of the editors could pick it up in Jefferson City during the session of the General Assembly. The Watsons' predecessor, Abel Rathbone Corbin, who had just retired from the quest for the Golden Fleece, appealed to his old subscribers to send money by their legislators, or to leave it with the postmasters in the various county seats, where he could collect it on a political trip through the state.[15]

Subscription prices tended to decline somewhat throughout the pioneer period, because of growing competition. Thus, early in the period, Charless charged three dollars in advance, or four dollars in country produce.[16] Stephen Remington required three dollars in advance, or four dollars at the end of the year, a more general practice among early newspaper editors.[17] By the 1840's the price had generally declined: William

Lusk asked $2.50 in advance, three dollars if paid within the year, and $3.50 if delayed longer, while R. H. Miller wanted two dollars if paid within six months and $2.50 if paid at the end of the year.[18] Samuel Clemens claimed that his brother Orion created one certainty when he reduced the prices of the *Hannibal Journal* from two dollars per year to one dollar in advance — he would never receive one cent of profit.[19]

While the published rates for advertising did not necessarily decline, editors did not demand payment in advance, and often, therefore, did not collect at all. The unit of measurement for advertising space, the square, lacked uniform dimensions among the print shops of the state. When he found collection difficult, the editor might take what he could get, although it might be considerably below his published rates.[20] By such means editors hoped to take business away from competing papers, and these practices continued until newspapers finally reached greater agreement on professional conduct.

III

Editors paid commissions to those willing to act as agents, to those who secured a stated number of subscribers, and to clubs which were willing to receive their newspaper in bulk. C. W. Todd and J. H. Middleton offered to send *The* (Boonville) *Western Emigrant* to groups of ten subscribers willing to receive it in a single package at $2.50 a newspaper, fifty cents below the normal price. An agent who obtained ten subscribers could choose between a free subscription for himself or a 10 per cent commission.[21] William Lusk gave a rate to clubs of five persons, who received five newspapers for the price of four. He solicited postmasters to act as agents, and promised such persons, whether postmasters or not, 10 per cent on all collections remitted within three months.[22] Such commissions were, of course, unnecessary for local subscribers, but constituted attempts to win patronage beyond the town of publication.

Editors appointed agents in all strategic towns where their

newspapers might circulate, whose duty it was to stimulate circulation and receive payments. Such agents could request reimbursement from subscribers, or possibly undertake to bring suit against perennial delinquents. Postmasters were asked to accept payment and to forward money to the editors. Nathaniel Patten, during and after his postmastership, served as agent for the *Missouri Gazette* in Howard and Cooper counties. Having received accounts of subscribers for collection, he notified them that suit would be commenced, unless they settled within a few days. T. J. Miller of the *St. Louis Times* sent a list of delinquent accounts to a lawyer, Abiel Leonard, to collect in the town of Fayette. If agreeable to Leonard, he was to keep 10 per cent and remit the balance to Miller.[23]

Still another method of forcing payment was a blacklist, which editors threatened to publish if accounts remained unsettled. The editors of the *Missouri Republican* announced that their blacklist contained two lawyers, three doctors, one writing master, four schoolmasters, one dancing master, and fifty gentlemen of no particular profession who had taken French leave.[24] Although editors warned that they would divulge names of citizens who were in arrears, they apparently rarely if ever lived up to their threat.

Thus the editor cajoled and threatened, but when it came time to deal personally with his patron, he generally moderated his approach. Here, perhaps, lay a fatal weakness. The editor published a schedule of advertising and subscription rates, but offered various concessions in individual cases. If the editor charged three dollars in advance, or four dollars at the end of the subscription year, he gladly settled for three dollars, whenever he could get it. He allowed himself to be hoodwinked time and again by transient advertisers, who inserted material in his columns without paying on first encounter. He permitted material to appear free of charge, which, strictly speaking, performed a service for the patron. He undertook job and book work, inserted notices, accepted subscriptions on credit, and charged no interest on overdue accounts. Somehow or other, he found that more people read his paper than subscribed, either through extensive borrowing, or by obtaining one free from him at the printing office. In brief, the editor had too many friends who imposed upon his good nature. No rule was rigid enough not to be broken at least once, and as long as he deviated from his stated terms whenever expediency seemed to require, his business relationships would remain unrewarding and unsatisfactory.[25]

IV

The number who subscribed to pioneer newspapers was never very impressive, in part because of the limitations imposed by the crude pioneer presses. Operating Charless' first printing press, two men could print seventy-five copies on one side in an hour. This may have been the same press, or a rebuilt form of it, on which Patten and Holliday published their first paper, or at least John T. Cleveland, a close associate of Patten's, thought so. In 1822 the *Missouri Republican* adopted a lever press which replaced the old Ramage screw press, and the same two men could print 125 newspapers in an hour. The Washington hand press was widespread, and was still in service in country establishments as late as the twentieth century. In 1837 the *Republican* installed an Adams power press, on which four hundred sheets an hour were printed, and in 1843 added a Hoe rotary, with a capacity of twelve hundred an hour.[26] But the use of the power press is not a part of our pioneer history.

Eastern newspapers often attained a circulation of more than one thousand, and if they achieved as much as four thousand, they had to go to press the day before delivery. Isaiah Thomas thought that a newspaper with six hundred subscribers and a fair amount of advertising could barely support itself.[27] In view of this estimate, Missouri newspapers lacked adequate patronage, as a rule. Charless began with a circulation of about 170 and only managed to survive with the aid of the public printing. He built up his subscription list to nearly one thousand, before he retired in 1821.[28] Patten was never satisfied with the length of his subscription list. In 1823 it had reached four hundred, apparently a considerable improvement over previous years. Perhaps it increased somewhat in later years, for Patten retired from his Columbia paper at least out of debt, though still in straitened circumstances.[29] James H. Middleton, of the Boonville *Western Emigrant*, claimed a reading public of between six and seven hundred.[30] In St. Louis, Charles Ramsey declared that the *New Era*, of which he was the printer, made money with four hundred subscribers and sixty yearly advertisers.[31] The circulation of the *Weekly California News* was only about 250 in its first year, a figure which Charles Keemle evidently thought adequate for a fledgling newspaper.[32] Most of the country newspapers did not attain the circulation figures of the more solid St. Louis newspapers, or of the *Jefferson Inquirer* or *Missouri Statesman*, both of which claimed a circulation of around two thousand in 1853.[33]

Many more people read newspapers than the subscription figures would show. The editor chafed in the knowledge that his newspaper passed from hand to hand, to be read by a large number of non-subscribers. Such a practice roused Nathaniel Patten's ire. "Sponging!" he derisively labeled it, and condemned so unfair and dishonorable a practice. In his opinion, one-half of Columbia's citizens depended upon the other half who subscribed, and he asked the non-subscribing half if they did not feel cheap.[34]

V

In the 1840's publishers adopted a somewhat tougher attitude toward the recalcitrant subscriber. This came from a growing demand on the part of editors to spell out personal and business relationships within the newspaper field. Although not until 1859 did the editors meet in convention to draw up

such a code,[35] many in the meantime published the "Law of
Newspapers," a list of rules which informed subscribers of their
obligations. These legal provisions were not based upon statute
law, but rested upon the more plastic common law where the
certainty of enforcement was less sure. Thus, while the following "Law of Newspapers" seemed to be severe upon subscribers,
it reflected newspaper grievances more than it protected
editors:

1. Subscribers who do not give express notice to the con-
   trary, are considered as wishing to continue their subscription.
2. If subscribers order the discontinuance of their periodicals, the publisher may continue to send them till
   all arrearages are paid and subscribers are responsible
   for all the numbers sent.
3. If subscribers neglect or refuse to take their periodical
   from the office to which they are directed, they are held
   responsible till they have settled their bills, and ordered
   them discontinued.
4. If subscribers remove to other places without informing
   the publishers, and their periodicals are sent to their
   former direction they are held responsible.
5. The Courts have decided that refusing to take a newspaper or *periodical* from the office, or removing and
   leaving it uncalled for until arrearages are paid, is
   prima facie evidence of intentional fraud.[36]

Others forsook legal threats for earnest entreaty. In Liberty, R. H. Miller suggested a ten-point program to subscribers
and patrons to better sustain a local paper. Written in 1859 at
the close of the pioneer period, his proposals had a timeliness
applicable to the whole era of frontier journalism. Miller first
urged the patron to lay aside all fears that the editor would ever
get rich. These fears aside, the patron's obligations were clear:
keep accounts paid in advance; encourage circulation among
all relatives and acquaintances living at a distance; avoid hag-
gling over printing rates; submit commercial and legal advertising (the last very lucrative) to the home-town newspaper;

patronize the country and not the city paper for labels, handbills and cards; do not expect frequent honorable mention in
editorial puffs; and do not dun the editor if he owes you, and
then sever the ties of friendship when you owe him. Lastly, Miller stated the Golden Rule, "Do unto others as you would have
them do unto you." [37] While Miller's program was ideally suited
to end the editor's financial woes, its fulfillment, like the Golden
Rule, was well-nigh impossible.

VI

As the pilot of a newspaper enterprise, then, the editor had
to be constantly on the alert against the spectre of failure which
pursued him down a rough and rocky road. Too often the editor
was in the same position as Joshua Norvell, who had relin-
quished control of the *Western Journal* and fled to Arkansas,
leaving Charles Lucas to collect back subscriptions and satisfy
creditors.[38] Others, like Charles Keemle or J. W. Denver, would
have struggled on, if they had not been so disappointed in the
paltry support of friends and partisans. Weary and toilsome
labor had endangered their health, and there seemed to be no
alternative to increasing financial indebtedness.[39] After thirty
years of editing, Thomas Watson stepped down from the helm
of the *Missouri Argus* for want of "that most efficient and de-
lightful of all kind of support — *paying the printer*." [40] For many
others it was a game of nip and tuck, and as one of them said,
they had been neither very high nor very low, pecuniarily or
otherwise.[41] Success crowned the achievements of a select
few, but these exceptions were rare. One wonders how most of
them kept body and soul together.

OUR OWN CONCERNS

𝒯HE PIONEER editor, when he occasionally wrote of his economic affairs, captioned his article "Our own Concerns" or "Our own Affairs." Here he would give clues about his business organization, financial affairs, postal problems, and labor conditions. He would also discuss the subscriber — mostly the delinquent subscriber, that ubiquitous creature who caused him so much anguish.

I

The business organization of the frontier press evolved from simple to more complex forms in the pioneer period. In the beginning the printer labored as much at the case and at the press as with pen and paper, performing all the basic operations of printer, editor, and publisher. He composed the type and ran the dampened newsprint off the hand press. He wrote much of his material, although the bulk of his paper was filled with advertisements, governmental pronouncements, reprints, and letters to the editor. He sought subscribers, but he probably did not hawk his newspaper, leaving the matter of distribution

97

to the mails, the newsboy, or pick-up at the printing office. He worried over his finances, striving to make both ends meet. He guided the public policies of the newspaper, weaving it into the political, religious, or literary fabric of society.

Over the years these functions of printer, editor, and publisher divided, and as the frontier receded, specialization set in. The distinction between the three was not always clearly defined, and rarely, except in the St. Louis newspapers, did all exist separately in one newspaper establishment.

In the printer-editor organization, the printer superintended the newspaper office, and the editor set general policy, wrote political pieces, and managed money affairs. In an editor-publisher type of organization, the typography and press work might be left to apprentices and journeymen. The editor was responsible for news and editorials, the publisher for economic affairs. The capital for an enterprise, in this case, came from the publisher (or proprietor as he was often called), or perhaps it came from an outside source at interest, perhaps from lenders who had political motives.

Always, however, in the frontier era, one could find the simple printer — struggling to get free of a creditor, clipping from other journals, composing at the case, assisting at the press, pleading with subscribers, ruining his health — and continuing to represent the simplest form of business organization until after the Civil War.

Nathaniel Patten, for example, lived as a struggling practical printer who managed, through many vicissitudes, barely to rise out of debt. He discontinued his Winchester *Kentucky Advertiser* in 1817 because of arrears in subscriptions.[1] Coming to Missouri, he issued a prospectus in February, 1819, and in March wrote to Secretary of State Adams to ask for the contract to print the laws of the United States in his *Missouri Intelligencer and Boon's Lick Advertiser*, which he said he had just established.[2] He had not, however, undertaken his enterprise with his own capital; this had been supplied by Benjamin Holliday, whose name appeared with Patten's on the masthead of the first issue, April 23.[3]

Holliday's investment probably made him no money, for a year later Patten was forced to sell his interest to Holliday for $450. Holliday still did not make money. He attempted twice to get out of the newspaper business, but his first effort to transfer the paper to John Payne did not succeed. During the two years' time that Holliday was the nominal publisher, Patten was the printer-editor. Holliday finally unloaded his burden upon its founder, Patten himself, who paid Holliday $1,200 to sever forever his connection with the paper.[4]

Patten had no money and borrowed enough to buy out Holliday — $1,100 from his mother in Boston, and $200 from John T. Cleveland. He paid his mother no interest, and mortgaged to her the log cabin which housed his printing establishment. To compensate Cleveland, Patten took him in as a business partner. Cleveland kept the books and received one-third of the profits.[5]

The new firm of Patten and Cleveland started out with renewed hopes of success. They purchased some needed equipment and issued a prospectus to attract additional patronage. Like other journalistic enterprises of the pioneer period, the firm was not incorporated, but operated under a simple partnership form of agreement.

This loosely-worded agreement, however, left so many questions in doubt that within two years the "co-partners" dissolved their contract in bitterness and recrimination. Cleveland, in an effort to recoup his investment, began collecting the debts due the firm. He so badgered and dunned balky and sensitive patrons that they stopped their subscriptions. The alarmed Patten publicly protested Cleveland's practice. He announced that he would not stop a subscription unless applied to personally. Cleveland responded by stopping his own subscription to the *Intelligencer* and by paying through an intermediary the twenty-five cents he owed for back numbers. Patten refused to print

Cleveland's letter of justification. He vowed never to mention Cleveland's name in the paper again.[6]

Still in debt, Patten slowly worked his way out, so that in 1828 he owed his mother only $340. Then a blow fell from which he never recovered. A thief had stolen $800 from him while he was postmaster at Franklin, and now the Post Office Department demanded remuneration. The theft occurred under almost fantastic circumstances. The thief had pulled the chest with the postal funds from under Patten's bed, slashed it open, and carried the money away. Patten, being deaf, never awakened. The money was never found, and Patten did not have money of his own with which to reimburse the Department.

Patten did everything possible to repay the loss. He dismissed his recently acquired editor, John Wilson, even though it was in the midst of the presidential campaign of 1828, and took over again all the functions of printer, editor, and publisher. This reduced expenses to a bare minimum. He borrowed the $800 at 10 per cent interest, mortgaged two lots, a female slave and her increase, and the equipment in his printing office. He paid off this loan only, in 1837, with his share and his sister's share of his mother's estate. He bargained for his sister's share, by transferring to her cash and property in Fayette.

Patten sought surcease from his financial woes through a congressional appropriation, but in this, as in all things, he met frustration. His bill for relief came up in Congress at least twelve times, but it always died a-borning. Once it failed by the vote of the Vice-President, and another time it passed the House, but in transferring the bill to the Senate, the papers were lost, and Patten had to wait for the next session of Congress. Patten watched ruefully, while Congress awarded James Monroe $37,000 and considered giving him $67,000 more. He watched while Senator Thomas Hart Benton and Representative W. H. Ashley allowed his bill to languish. After his death, his wife and son vainly petitioned Congress twice for relief, pleading dire need as the justification for their request. The tes-

timony and reports in these congressional documents give valuable insights into the character of Patten: his deafness, his
industriousness and conscientiousness, his good reputation
among his fellow citizens, and the poor circumstances under
which he departed this life in 1837.[7]

After the crisis of 1828 — not only a financial, but a political
debacle as well — Patten conducted the paper alone. Early in
1835 he advertised for a practical printer without capital, who
would share with him the profits of the establishment. Finding
none, he sold his paper to James S. Rollins, Sinclair Kirtley, and
Thomas Miller, who employed a practical printer and renamed
the paper *The Columbia Patriot.* They bought the paper for
$800 (not including the office building), to be paid in two
yearly installments. Patten was to deliver the paper when the
first installment was paid in December.[8]

When Patten left his stand in Columbia he planned no new
ventures, yet printer's ink ran so thick in his veins that he was
soon at the business again. With Alphonso Wetmore, a frontier
author of some note, he projected a commercial and literary
paper for St. Louis, the *St. Louis Memoir,* in which partisanship
and personal conflict were to be excluded. The venture never
got farther than the prospectus, however, and Patten established, instead, the *St. Charles Clarion* in November, 1836.[9] A
year later he died, leaving his wife and young son in extreme
want. Such were the fortunes of one pioneer editor, who found
the rigors of a tough, undeveloped frontier environment almost
overwhelming.

II

Though often obscured by undefined and fuzzy concepts, the
separate functions of printer, editor, and publisher can be dimly
seen in Patten's various business relationships. Further illustration of the executive structure of newspaper enterprise need
only be selective to suggest the types of business organization.
Like Nathaniel Patten, Joseph Charless and Calvin Gunn were

two printers who combined all three functions into one and captained their enterprise under their own initiative.[10]

Gunn first gained control of a newspaper through a mortgage on Robert M'Cloud's printing establishment in St. Charles. M'Cloud, a stepson of Joseph Charless and an unsuccessful printer, lost his equipment to Gunn in a lawsuit. Gunn then started the *Jeffersonian Republican* in 1824.[11] Later, after he had moved with the legislature to Jefferson City, the Democrats attempted to buy him out, or to persuade him to enlarge his paper by taking in a business partner, but Gunn, although a Jacksonian Democrat, resisted any efforts to relinquish his control into the hands of the party.[12]

Unlike Charless, Gunn, and Patten, other printers failed to achieve financial and personal independence from creditors and politicians, and were forced to divide the executive functions by accepting publishers or proprietors. A "military junto," with the thousand dollars it had raised, employed Joshua Norvell and Sergeant Hall to set up opposition papers to Joseph Charless. Doubtless this same faction underwrote another anti-Charless organization, the Isaac N. Henry and Company, which handled the affairs of the *St. Louis Enquirer*.[13] In the same manner, a group of men called the Hill Faction founded the *Missouri Republican* in 1822, and placed Edward Charless, son of Missouri's first pioneer editor, in charge.[14] Charles Keemle's *St. Louis Beacon* had a silent proprietor in the person of a Mr. Kennerly, who loaned money to the newspaper.[15] Orion Clemens, brother of Samuel, bought the *Hannibal Journal* for five hundred dollars, which he borrowed from an old farmer at 10 per cent interest.[16] These underwriters were not formally engaged in the actual publishing process.

Printers often entered formal partnerships when obtaining financial support. Patten did so, and so did Tubal E. Strange and Stephen Remington. Strange joined Dr. Zenas Priest in publishing the *Missouri Herald*. Remington at first had Minor M. Whitney and William Creath as partners, under the firm name of

Remington and Company, but when they terminated this business arrangement, he associated himself with James Russel. When they dissolved this partnership by mutual consent, Russel collected all debts due the establishment.[17] In such cases, the investor shared profits with the printer instead of receiving interest on the loaned money.

Partnership obligations varied widely, both as to duties and capital amounts invested. In a great many instances, all partners participated directly in the publication of the newspaper. Some lacked training as printers, but devoted full time to editorial functions, or, if the enterprise were large enough, looked after other aspects of the business. In senior-junior partnerships, the junior editor shared profits with the major owner on the basis of his contributions in the form of labor, and sometimes also through partial ownership of the firm. He performed more menial duties than the senior editor, and he often directly supervised the printing shop. Equal partnerships, in which two or more men associated on equal terms, were not uncommon.

III

It is clear that though the value of the initial capital investment in a pioneer newspaper was not large, the practical printer usually needed some outside partner, in order to set himself up in business. Patten freed himself from subservience to Benjamin Holliday for the sum of twelve hundred dollars, but seven years later would not sell to James H. Birch for $1,610.[18] For the information of Governor Daniel Dunklin, who along with his Jacksonian partisans was looking into the possibility of establishing a Democratic press, Charles Keemle listed the necessary articles he possessed for setting up a paper. Originally these materials cost two thousand dollars, he averred, but he would sell them for one thousand, one-third down, and the balance in three and nine months with interest. Significantly, he had no takers.[19] Curtis P. Anderson and Charles Groll bought printing materials for the *Weekly California News* at a cost of about eight hundred dollars.[20] A proprietor of the Fayette *Boon's Lick Times* offered to sell his half interest in the paper for five hundred dollars.[21] One Missouri newspaper, the *Jefferson Inquirer*, which utilized several power presses and issued a daily during legislative sessions, and thus hardly qualified as a pioneer newspaper, had $10,500 offered for its purchase, but this was several thousand below the price which the owners, the Lusks, considered acceptable.[22]

Determined to establish the first newspaper in Boonville, and "repeatedly urged, by their friends," James Middleton and William Need secured printing materials for the *Boonville Herald* from the Baltimore Type Foundry for $763.50, four hundred dollars of which was a mortgage to the type foundry. As time for publication neared, Middleton and Need remitted three hundred dollars cash against the $763.50, money which probably came from an outside investor. In further need of materials, the editors of the *Herald* very shortly increased their debt by $101.81. Then, as so often happened to the first pioneer journal in a frontier community, the *Herald* failed as a business enterprise. Three years after its beginning, in computing purchases, interest, and remittances, Middleton still owed the type foundry $629.56. By 1839 Middleton had worked with several different partners, but his debt, with accrued interest at 6 per cent, had increased to $727.09. The Baltimore Type Foundry did not wish to press him to insolvency, and instead brought suit in the Cooper County Circuit Court for part of the amount against Middleton's erstwhile partner, Robert Brent. The agent of the foundry instructed Abiel Leonard to use his own good judgment in the matter of Middleton's share of the debt, and apparently the editor paid part of the outstanding account.[23] The columns of Middleton's newspaper, then called *The Western Emigrant*, gave evidence of his financial difficulties, when he advertised his desire to sell a one-half interest in his establishment. He evidently sought a successor to Brent, and announced this opportunity as a chance for speculation.[24]

Thus the original capital outlay for a pioneer newspaper was at least six or seven hundred dollars. If a printer had published his newspaper for a number of years, however, he generally demanded a larger sum for his equipment and subscription list.

The operating costs of a newspaper establishment are difficult to determine, since so much depended on the extent of circulation, the size of the paper, the amount of new typesetting required for each issue, and various other indeterminate factors. In 1810 the cost of publishing each weekly issue of Charless' *Missouri Gazette* was twenty dollars. Forty-eight years later, its lineal descendant, the *Missouri Republican*, now a big city daily, spent four thousand dollars per week.[25] In 1836, Corbin explained that he paid forty dollars a week for eight or nine compositors, pressmen, and foremen.[26] Charles Keemle's weekly expenses for the *St. Louis Beacon* were at least fifty dollars in 1831.[27] Because the pioneer editor kept inadequate records, or none at all, arriving at any accurate estimate of his operating costs is impossible.

Before 1834 all printing supplies had to be purchased out of state — from type foundries in Cincinnati, Philadelphia, or Baltimore. In 1834, Lamme, Keiser and Company established a paper mill in Boone County, and in 1840 a type foundry was established in St. Louis.[28] But such local suppliers were often unreliable. Throughout the pioneer period publishers continued to patronize Eastern business houses. Type foundries stocked presses, type, ink in barrels, paper by the ream, and all the other paraphernalia of a printing office — cases, brass rule, ball skins, rollers, and stereotype plates and tools for zalographic engraving. Such firms accepted old type in partial payment for the new, gave a 5 per cent discount for cash, and extended six months' credit without interest.[29]

Not all printing offices were outfitted with new equipment directly from the foundry. When an editor wished to replace old materials with new, or when he wished to quit business, he offered his equipment for sale to printers in the interior. An-

nouncing his intention to purchase new type with which to publish the *Inquirer,* James Lusk advertised to printers that he
could outfit a neat and substantial country office for one-half
what it would cost in the East.[30]

IV

Since subscriptions and advertisements often failed to support an enterprise properly, printers also published handbills,
circulars, broadsides, orations, sermons, almanacs, gazetteers,
minutes of public meetings, books and texts, legal blanks, and
laws and official proceedings of the various governments. Before
statehood, editors restricted imprints mostly to handbills and
circulars. They also published the volumes of official laws and
journals of the territory and an occasional oration, sermon, or
broadside. Joseph Charless proposed to publish in one volume
A Narrative of the Indian War in the West and South in 1814, in
which he undoubtedly would have revealed his anti-Indian bias
and depicted the red man as a mere "appendage to the human
family." [31] An unknown publisher printed the broadside of
John Cleves Symmes, setting forth his theory of the concentric
sphere, in which he described the earth as hollow and opened
at the poles, and staked his life on the truth of his statement.
Other examples of printing, besides the public printing, were
Charless' Missouri and Illinois Almanac, an oration of Frederick
Bates, the Articles of Association of the Missouri Fur Company,
a political piece in which Charles Lucas defended himself
against John Scott, sermons of Salmon Giddings, and minutes of
the Bethel Baptist Association.

After 1821 the range of subjects widened to include survey-
ing, poetry, and drama, but religious, political, and economic
subjects received the heaviest emphasis. Sermons, minutes of
religious associations, political orations, gazetteers, and annual
commercial surveys were frequently printed. Throughout the
pioneer period, public printing constituted a large and profit-
able sideline to the newspaper publisher. Some print shops

were devoted exclusively to book and job work. Newspaper editors probably thought of this more as a sideline, except, perhaps, Charles Keemle, whose newspaper enterprises seem to have been subservient to his Book and Job Printing Office.[32]

V

Vital to the business operations of a newspaper, as well as to its makeup, was the mail service provided by the United States government. No editor depended entirely on his local community for the total circulation of his paper. He encouraged a regional, if not state-wide, coverage, which depended on regular and efficient mail facilities. But though the Post Office Department established post roads and let mail contracts as each new community was established, mail service was poor.

Joseph Charless early set the pattern for later editors to follow, when he registered a protest against the "blunders of this man" (the postrider) who had "disgusted the people so." [33] In a personal letter to Postmaster-General R. J. Meigs, he urged that prompt and effectual measures be taken to prevent a repetition of mail failures in the St. Louis area.[34]

Regulations of the Post Office Department placed a heavy burden of obligation upon the postmasters, who had to count newspapers wrapped in a packet, collect postage from subscribers (since publishers did not prepay), notify printers when newspapers remained in the post office uncalled for, and, where possible, forward mail when subscribers had moved. Many of the postmasters, no doubt, were a lackadaisical lot who failed to fulfill these regulations. Editors did not let them off lightly for jeopardizing a segment of their business.

Some of the difficulties of mail transmission were attendant upon the very rigors of the wilderness itself: bad roads, Indian attacks, and lonely distances. These forced unannounced alterations in time schedules. Human failures were responsible for other failures as well. The newspapers in transit were not easily handled by postal employees. They were so bulky that post-

riders often left them behind, and they were thrown off the
stagecoaches to make room for passengers. Subscribers often
received them in damaged condition. Editors frequently sent
them off while still dampened for the impression, and to further
plague the postal employee, wrappers often came unglued,
leaving the paper open and hard to manage. Although the Post
Office Department provided a fine for any employee who
opened a newspaper to read, the practice seemed a fairly common occurrence.[35]

Newspapers did not pay their way in the postal service, con-
stituting about fourteen-fifteenths of the weight of all mail
moved in 1832, but bringing only one-ninth of the revenue.
Postal rates varied, somewhat, over the pioneer period. The Act
of 1798 set a rate of one cent for one hundred miles or less and
one and one-half cents for any mileage over a hundred. In
1825 an act allowed circulation within a state for one cent, re-
gardless of the distance. In the Act of 1845, when the postal
department began to take into consideration factors of weight
and size, newspapers of nineteen hundred square inches or less
could be sent free, within a thirty-mile radius of place of publication. Because of the laxity of postmasters, printers were often
able to send many journals beyond that distance free. But when
the Postmaster-General devised a plan whereby each printer
had to certify the number of papers sent, and the postmaster
had to secure the postage three months in advance, a 50 per cent
increase in revenue resulted.[36]

As long as there was a weekly or even semi-weekly mail delivery, publishers varied the date of publication to suit the
times of arrival and departure. Editors depended on arrivals
to gather from other journals and from letters intelligence from
the East, and on departures to dispatch their own newspapers
just off the press to their distant subscribers. For the editor, the
facts of the mail timetable governed the choice of publication
day, and any alteration, irregularity, or peculiarity of the schedule occasioned change, and sometimes anguish, on that day.

VI

If the editor as a capitalist and business manager suffered ill fortune, his travail as a labor manager was no less troublesome. Although apprentices and journeymen were still to be found in a print shop, the old craft system was beginning to break down. No longer did prestige attach to the master printer as it once had. Journeymen could not graduate into full-fledged printer status unless they had private capital or a good business connection. As for the indenture system, it received into it objects of charity, children who had come under the purview of the county court and who did not necessarily intend to learn a specific trade and to work out the long apprenticeship. As a result of the instability within the printing craft, conditions of labor were hardly satisfactory to either employer or employee.

The Missouri legislature laid down rules under which all indentures were to be made. Over the whole relationship between master and apprentice, the county court had a controlling hand. It might hear complaints of both masters and apprentices, and might, if circumstances required, dissolve a contract.[37]

In the print shop the apprentice performed mostly menial tasks, but he could fairly quickly learn how to set "straight" matter, after which he might run off and hire himself out at a wage. Negroes were sometimes hired to perform various tasks. They reverted back to their masters at the end of the hiring period.

When the printer advertised for an apprentice, he asked usually that he be fourteen to sixteen years of age, although Joseph Charless once lowered the qualifying age to ten years.[38] All printers wanted applicants of good, steady, moral, and industrious habits. "No other need apply."[39] In return, the printer promised to pay every attention to the boy's morals and to give him board and clothing. One suspects that the master waived the obligation to teach his charge to read and write or to send him to school. As in the other trades, the apprentice had a habit of absconding, and when Edward Charless of the *Missouri Re-*

publican advertised for a runaway, he offered only one cent reward, a sufficient recompense for one so indolent and careless.[40]

The editor relied most upon his journeyman printer, who had already acquired the various skills of newspaper work and could gather the type into the composing stick, impose it onto the stone table, lock it up in the case, and operate the press. The more skillful and dependable the journeyman printer, the more freedom the editor could have from the mechanical labors of publishing a newspaper. Joseph Charless advertised for a journeyman printer to take charge of a printing office about to be erected in a neighboring village, thus placing a great reliance upon a mere wage earner.[41] Since a number of editors were not printers and had not learned the trade, we may assume that the actual task of publication was often left in the hands of these craftsmen of the print shop. Charles Keemle acted in this capacity for Isaac Henry and Thomas Hart Benton, of the *St. Louis Enquirer.*[42]

Journeymen received their wages by the week or by the piece. Charless advertised in 1812 for a young, white man of orderly habits (a gambler or a drunkard need not apply) to receive instruction that would enable him to earn eight dollars a week in any of the cities of the Atlantic. In 1817 he offered twenty-five dollars a month, with room, board, and laundry added, to a swift compositor.[43] Perhaps wages declined in the pioneer period, for more than twenty years later Abel Rathbone Corbin paid each of nine compositors, pressmen, and foremen three or four dollars a week.[44] When Orion Clemens employed his brother, Samuel, on the *Hannibal Journal*, he promised to pay him three and a half dollars a week, which Samuel termed an extravagant wage. But, due to Orion's way of doing business, not one cent of it was ever paid.[45] Patten stated that journeymen's wages formed a heavy item in the expense of a printing office.[46] Probably, even in a country print shop, a two dollar weekly wage would have been low, and in the more prosperous newspaper establishments, from three to four dollars was acceptable.

Workers occasionally caused editors much trouble. After Joseph Charless established the *Gazette* in St. Louis, he returned to Louisville to terminate his business and family concerns and left the paper in the hands of Jacob Hinkle, who botched affairs so thoroughly that he fled when Charless came back. The indignant Charless printed a notice warning against Hinkle and advertised for another journeyman printer to work at the case. Twenty years after Charless' death, Hinkle brazenly took credit for setting up the first press in St. Louis.[47] Nathaniel Patten had similar trouble with one of his employees, James S. Linn. While employed on the *Intelligencer*, James H. Birch of the *Western Monitor* had called Linn a liar and a scoundrel. For some reason, however, Linn left Patten's employ. Birch, seizing every opportunity to discredit Patten, took Linn under his wing. Among other things, Linn and Birch haled Patten into court for overdue wages, and the whole experience only added to Patten's burden of growing troubles.[48]

The quality of labor which printers attracted to their shops was not always high, and because of the mutual distrust and suspicion between master and employee, labor-management relations were permeated with bad feelings and unfulfilled contracts. Apparently there was a large turnover in the staff of a newspaper. The master employer gave to his laborer as little as he possibly could, and the worker reciprocated with slovenliness, dishonesty, and intemperance, as well as unscheduled departures from the office. Not only must he cope with frontier inconveniences unknown to his brethren in the East, complained Patten, but he also had to pay the highest wages for the worst workmen, and frequently, because of their itinerant habits, he was left to carry on alone.[49]

But printer-employers themselves were not above reproach. Samuel Clemens described his treatment at the hands of J. P. Ament, of the *Hannibal Courier*. When Sam's father died, he was taken from school and apprenticed to the printer's trade. Ament allowed him the usual emolument — board and clothing, but he skimped on both, giving Sam only one of his old castoff suits, so much too large for him that he felt as if he were in a circus tent. Since the food was inadequate and lacked variety he and Wales McCormick stole potatoes from the cellar at night, despite the fact that Ament moved the two from the kitchen to the family table. Mrs. Ament guarded every morsel of food closely, even sweetened the coffee herself, and Sam and Wales were convinced she wet the spoon first before she put it in the sugar.

The antics of this duo illustrate the lack of responsibility which workmen sometimes displayed. When the great Reverend Alexander Campbell came to preach, Wales and Sam had to print his sermon. However, they used the initials "J. C." for Jesus Christ, manifestly an unsatisfactory abbreviation to the Reverend, who, as they expected, returned with the sermon to the office, where "his countenance cast a gloom over the whole place." Having to enlarge the name and reset the whole type, the two apprentices lengthened the Savior's name to Jesus H. Christ.[50] We may only surmise how this affected the preacher's grim visage.

Evidence of the delinquency of apprentices is the pious advice editors sometimes passed out to them. Labor was a blessing, they were told, and an apprentice would do well to study and be industrious. A few extra steps in the print shop were of greater value to the apprentice than he, perhaps, realized. If he would pass his apprenticeship happily he should always be careful to consult the wishes of the master, and if he lived in the family, he should always seek to please the lady of the house. The apprentice had only to satisfy the heads of the family that he was determined to merit their good opinion, and he was sure to obtain it.[51]

Despite the editor's unhappiness with his working force, he relied upon it for an indispensable portion of the labors of a print shop. Patten missed an issue and printed on a half sheet during most of January, 1831, because of an accident to one of his workmen.[52] And Joseph Charless, in his desire to cater to the French population of St. Louis, advertised in French for a native of France as an apprentice, to learn to set type in his own tongue.[53]

VII

The working force of a newspaper establishment carried on its labors amidst apparent chaos and confusion. Famous for its lack of order and decorum, the print shop presented to the eye of the uninitiated a cluttered array of type fonts, imposing stones, the press, hell drawers, printing tools, and reams of paper. A layman who was asked to "fix up the hash" while the editor was out of town described an office in this way!

> Here is a great iron concern with big bars, levers, rollers and screws, standing exactly in the middle of the floor, occupying just twice as much room as it would anywhere else, and looking far better suited for a machine shop, than a young literary emporium. Then there are papers of all sizes from a seven-by-nine, up to a mammoth, scattered all around the room and tables, just as if a young whirlwind had been frolicking among them. Then such a paraphernalia — a deformed inkstand, an empty wafer box, an old rusty steel pen, a big bottle with something green in it, (we never have learned what it is) a big pair of shears which we are told bears the very respectful title of "assistant editor."[54]

The print shop was, then, labyrinthine confusion to the novice. Such chaos perhaps corresponded to the troubled finances and labor problems of the pioneer editor.

CHAPTER 8

AMONG OUR EDITORIAL
BRETHREN

$\mathcal{A}$s a profession, the editorial corps was not bound together by any tight rules of discipline or an accepted code of etiquette. Editors felt at liberty to criticize their fellow editors even to the point of abuse, and editorial relationships were marred frequently by violence and altercations. As a matter of fact, newspapering could hardly yet be considered a profession, but it had taken steps in this direction by the eve of the Civil War.

Tocqueville noted the lack of discipline and unity of action among the journalists of the United States. The intense competition among American newspapermen led each of the editors to fight under his own standard. Tocqueville distinguished this as the chief characteristic of the American press — an open and coarse appeal to the passions of readers and assaults upon the characters of individuals.[1] A spirit of combat militated against the formation of professional standards. So long as this extreme individualism existed among journalists, so long as they attacked each other with a vengeance, standards remained low.

I

From the outset the pioneer editor adopted as axiomatic the idea that all other editors were fair game for pursuit. To all who questioned Joseph Charless' criticisms of rival editors, he replied that the political opinions of a newspaper editor were legitimate subjects of discussion, and any heretical doctrines or wrongful opinions must be combated and corrected.[2] Likewise, Lucian J. Eastin told the readers of the *Jefferson Inquirer* that he would expose all errors and inconsistencies of his editorial brethren.[3]

So saying, the editors let fly their slings and arrows. Largely politically inspired, these volleys often did not stop with words, but went to libel suits and even physical combat. Some of the criticisms were not intemperate, of course, but often they were.

Calvin Gunn was more easy going than most of his editorial brethren who carried on sustained campaigns of vituperation. While Gunn accused other editors of culpable remissness, he too often weakened his critiques by gentle barbs and pungent sarcasm that stirred his adversaries risibilities, rather than their wrath. Under the head of "Editorial Difficulties," for instance, he attacked Adam Block Chambers of the *Salt River Journal* as a Federalist. What, gentle reader, should be done with this queer, hypocritical journal! He also attacked the *Boonville Herald* for its Federalism, but he diminished the sting of his thrust, by calling it a "hebdomedal" (i.e., that which occurs every seven days). He commented satirically on the anguish of Nathaniel Patten of the *Missouri Intelligencer*, who believed that legislators were not nearly so tall as in the days when Putnam shot a wolf in the caves of Pomfret. He good-naturedly castigated other editors, pointing out their sorrows and distresses, and concluding with the hope that a few readers would send him ("post paid — mark that friend") a solution to these editorial difficulties.[4]

Most editors were not so tender-minded as Gunn and attacked their fellow editors in all seriousness. Joseph Charless unfairly impugned the honesty of his rival, Sergeant Hall, and when Hall countercharged, Charless pronounced his arguments as "either false in point of fact, or so weak and absurd as to resemble more the tales of children or women." [5] Charless' unsparing attacks reached a climax when he put the following satirical words in Editor Hall's mouth:

> People of Missouri, I have been brought here by a faction, who represent the country as ready to receive a federal stamp, or any impression they choose to give it. They as well as myself, feel our mistake — and have sent me to work, to *lie* down the *Gazette*. I fasten on every paragraph in that paper, with all the venom of a viper, yet I cannot procure support — oh! do my good people, come on, and subscribe to the Emigrant, as my present list will not defray the expense of the paper which *I give away* to serve the cause I am engaged in. [6]

As if to answer this slander, Hall's successor on the renamed *St. Louis Enquirer*, Thomas Hart Benton, inserted a jingle on the editor of the *Gazette*:

> Spleen to mankind his canker'd heart posses't
> And much he hated all, but most the best;
> "*The Enquirer man*" his everlasting theme,
> And filthy scandal his delight supreme. . . .
> Pope, Jr.[7]

Probably the most famous of the editorial combats occurred from 1827 to 1830 in Fayette between Nathaniel Patten and James H. Birch, a contest in which Patten was an unequal combatant. Members of the profession generally agreed that Birch was the most reckless and abusive of the Missouri editors. [8] He often goaded Patten into excesses, despite Patten's better judgment. In the beginning Patten earnestly and piously justified his course before the onslaughts of Birch, who, however, denounced Patten's motives on every occasion. Finally, Patten retaliated in kind. From his refuge in Columbia he declared that Birch had hydrophobia, inflicted by the bite of a pole-cat. "He foams and raves in all the phrenzy of *madness*." [9]

In time, Birch got another rival in the person of William B. Napton of the *Boon's Lick Democrat*. When Patten saw the prospectus for this newspaper in his old stand, he predicted a *"regular Kilkenny cat fight"* between the two rival editors, the brothers Birch and Napton.[10]

In another village, R. H. Miller was enraged when he read in the opposition paper, the Liberty *Democratic Platform*, criticism of his understanding of *quo warranto* proceedings in the circuit court. Highly sensitive to censure, he clawed away at this blackguard, this

> miserable hireling editor of the Platform . . . the dirty tool of a set of worthless, unprincipled and law defying men. . . . He resembles in his nature and in his taste a certain species of the feathered tribe — a venerable looking bird of dark and sable plumage, that is often seen wheeling in the heavens in search of tainted air, and delighting especially to dwell in an atmosphere loaded with the stench of putrid carcasses . . . beware lest you one day wear the brand of the State of Missouri, which is a smooth shave off of one side of the head and a broad stripe down one side of the breeches leg.[11]

Editors, it seemed, could not separate an attack upon their political principles from an attack upon their personal motives. A criticism of one was a criticism of the other. Although strictures of opposition political tenets should have been perfectly legitimate, the debate sooner or later got around to character assassination. Since newspapers were moral agents, and questions were considered in terms of right and wrong, a charge of inconsistency was especially galling to an editor. His stand on the issues of the day, he believed, was founded on objectivity. In a parting word to his subscribers, Abel Rathbone Corbin affirmed that his sound and independent opinions had "been so formed and so expressed, as to stand the test of time and truth." [12]

After editorial combat had reached its apogee, the pioneer journalist sometimes struck the name of his opponent from his columns and his exchange list. Charless banished Benton's name from the *Gazette*, although he made unmistakable allusions to him. In return, Benton ostensibly stopped reading the *Gazette*. Charless published the following short letter: "Mr. Joseph Charless will discontinue my subscription to his newspaper," signed by Thomas Hart Benton, and thus his name appeared in print after all.[13]

W. F. Birch of the *Western Monitor* erased the *Salt River Journal* and the *Boonville Herald* from his exchange list. The *Journal*, not knowing what had "stirred the *Monitor's* bile, to overflowing" did the same, and also struck the name of Birch from its columns forever. The *Herald*, chagrined because Birch had charged it with a lack of editorial honor and dignity, had already dropped the *Monitor*, and cried out in anguish against this "renegade from Kentucky — is it for *him* to lecture the Editorial fraternity of Missouri about the dignity of the profession? God forbid!"[14]

As a part of editorial conflict, newspapers often adopted a supercilious attitude toward each other. This seemed to be true of the conservative press in Missouri, and it certainly was so of the two leading Whig papers in the state. Charless and Paschall, or Patten, would haughtily refuse to take notice of an opposition press, or picayunishly publicize every typographical error to discredit the status of a rival. Noticing the short-lived *St. Louis Courier*, a Jackson paper, the *Missouri Republican* quoted verbatim its spelling of "buplic [*sic*] opinion," and promised to reprint such "chaste and perfect specimens of writing" from the *Courier* which would come into vogue, it was sure, after Old Hickory's inauguration.[15]

The *Republican's* attitude of looking down its nose often sent Abel Rathbone Corbin of the *Missouri Argus* into paroxysms of rage. Quoting the remark, "We are not in the habit of answering, or taking any notice whatever of the editorial articles of the Argus," Corbin denounced the *Republican* for presuming dignity at the expense of his paper.[16] Though the *Republican* did not deign to notice the *Argus*, the *Argus* pledged itself "to bestow upon *it* [the *Republican*] *our special consideration*." Derisively, Corbin credited Charless and Paschall with slender abilities, feeble literary efforts, and incapacity for anything but the superintendence of the manual labor of their establishment. No two men could be capable of pouring forth "such a continued stream of low, dirty, insinuations and rancorous invective."[17]

Patten also treated his opponents with aloofness. He announced it was unnecessary to trouble his readers any further about editorials in Calvin Gunn's *Jeffersonian*, "a little self-important demi-sheet," a reference to Gunn's frequent printing on a half-sheet. Of James Birch's editorial efforts, he liked especially to point out faults, not only typographical errors, but misinformation as well. Birch's execution of the public printing, he charged, was done in a slovenly, incorrect, and unworkmanlike manner.[18] Even though Patten, ever the conscience of Missouri pioneer journalism, wished to raise the standards of his craft and profession, his own criticisms of his colleagues illustrated the lack of cooperation among his editorial brethren which prevented the establishment of a unifying code of ethics and practice.

Many editors called for a halt to scurrility and pugnaciousness. Patten constantly decried the abusiveness, censure, and slander among the editorial brethren.[19] Corbin questioned the necessity of it, and doubted that severity toward one another was right, or creditable to the profession. He called upon Birch, believed to be the most intemperate, to lead in the reform.[20] Though they may have had their tongues in cheek, the editors of the *Boon's Lick Democrat*, the *Jeffersonian Republican*, and the *Missouri Argus* piously declared that the language of the *Missouri Republican* hurt the reputation of Missouri in the East. The *Republican*, because of its prominence as the outstanding newspaper in the state, represented a low level of culture to arrogant and officious moralists, who descended upon Missouri to reconstruct its supposedly crude and vulgar populace. Such misconduct of the *Republican*, in imputing rudeness and crassness to Missourians, should not go unreproved, commented Calvin Gunn.[21]

Stimulated by the rise of competition, editors hurled their shafts of abuse with increasing frequency. As long as an editor had no rivals in his territory, he kept rancor and invective at a minimum. But let another newspaper be established, and a ruthless and even ruinous competition inevitably ensued. The threat of a reduced subscription list drove the editor to unusual exertions. Subscribers were hard to find in the first place; to divide them with another newspaper meant even more meager financial returns.[22]

On the first hint of a rival paper, Charless cried out in anguish. He claimed a junto conspired to destroy freedom of the press and starve him out because he had criticized the military during the war. He described the motives of his opponents, under the title "Spirit of Intolerance":

> Am I then to be proscribed, when I merely exercise that right which I possess in common with my fellow citizens, and point out abuses with which government could not otherwise possibly become acquainted.[23]

Other editors expressed opposition to rivals in their areas. Even an increase within the state filled the country editor with foreboding.[24] Patten feared not only the St. Louis press, but also the eastern journals. He could view the multiplication of presses only with mixed feelings. On the one hand, this could be viewed as indicative of increasing population, wealth, and intelligence. On the other, he dubbed it "Newspaper Mania." He described the St. Louis market as overstocked with newspapers in 1835. He declined to become the agent of the *Philadelphia Journal*, for he would not encourage the diversion of patronage to eastern newspapers; he had already suffered too much by it. After stressing that every additional newspaper establishment decreased his subscription list, he appealed to every citizen of Boone County to patronize his press.[25]

Editors in general opposed the reduction or abolition of postage on newspapers, because the prevailing desire of people in the country to read city papers would drive the local papers out of business unless they could circulate more cheaply in the interior.[26] Patten greeted with approval the refusal of Congress to lower newspaper postage. Although it might help his own circulation, he feared eastern competition much more.[27]

II

Requirements for admission into the editorial fraternity were nonexistent. Without any prerequisites for admission, professionalization of the occupation was virtually impossible, and many entered it who had no training whatever as journalists. The true pioneer editor was a practical printer who believed that *all* editors should go through the novitiate of apprentice and journeyman as he had done. But such was not to be. Editors found their field crowded by lawyers, politicians, preachers, merchants, businessmen, land speculators, surveyors, and even a blacksmith.

The practical printers were incensed when Benjamin Lawhead, a blacksmith, invaded the printing profession and underbid them for the public printing of the State of Missouri. Gunn, who had expected to win the contract, was crestfallen. Though he avowed no feelings of disappointment or envy of Lawhead, he maintained that the dignity of the profession would continue to suffer and the contracts for the public printing would be executed in a slipshod fashion, unless the old proverb, "Every man to his trade," gained acceptance.[28]

Here was one matter on which Nathaniel Patten could agree with his political opponent, the editor of the *Jeffersonian*. A grave injustice had been done to professional printers. He disliked, especially, the common practice of awarding the public printing to lawyers who had presses under their control and looked to party chieftains for promotion. This practice robbed the poor printers of what justly belonged to them, and now was the time to take a stand — a spirited protest to the state legislature. When had a lawyer-printer fulfilled his contract on time, or according to specifications? When Patten first saw Lawhead's product, he could say it was handsomely bound but only *tolerably* well printed.[29]

So indignant were the Missouri editors with Lawhead as public printer that he defended himself in the columns of the *Missouri Argus*. Not only had Whig editors, such as Charless and Paschall of the *Missouri Republican*, criticized his typography, but fellow Democratic editors harangued him, as well. His great sin, he admitted, was in being a blacksmith and not a printer.[30] Although his critics did not seem to be aware of it, Lawhead was evidently closely connected with Corbin of the *Missouri Argus*. He may, indeed, have been a front man for the Jacksonian editor.[31]

Lawhead demonstrated the ease and informality with which non-printers could enter the trade. And just as non-printers entered the trade, so also printers had sidelines in non-printing trades. Postmaster, justice of the peace, land speculator, apothecary — these were some of the sidelines in which printers engaged.

III

The editor was in many respects like other figures on the frontier. He lacked professional status, he bore the bitter criticism of his colleagues, he competed intensely both politically and economically, and he was a jack-of-all trades. Another trait he shared in common with other frontiersmen was itineracy. Not all editors moved about with unrestrained ease, but enough of them did so as to lend an aura of mobility to the whole editorial profession.

There were several reasons for the itineracy of the frontier editor. The old cliché about the printer starting a paper with a press and only "a shirttail full of type" was vivid expression of the fact that little capital outlay was necessary to establish a paper. But when the easily established papers failed, as they did frequently, the editors were forced to move on. Then, too, the very restiveness and fluidity of frontier society contributed to the wanderlust of the editors.

A pioneer editor most notable for his itinerant ways was Lucian J. Eastin. Born in Kentucky, he learned his craft in Lexington. His Missouri career began in 1836, on the *Missouri Argus*. Thereafter he edited no less than twelve newspapers, not only in Missouri, but also in Wisconsin, Iowa, Kansas, and Nebraska. Although he had had a checkered career on many newspapers — he was known as a "red hot" Jacksonian editor — he held the esteem of his fellow editors and was known among them as the Nestor of the Missouri Press. Elected president of the Missouri Press Association in 1875, he died in the following year.[32]

An itinerant printer of a little different sort, Charles Keemle, moved not from town to town editing newspapers, but from newspaper to newspaper in St. Charles and St. Louis. Born in 1800 in Philadelphia, he served his apprenticeship in Norfolk, Virginia. Coming to Vincennes, he established the *Indiana Centinel* with Samuel Dillworth in 1817. But in a very short time he had moved on to St. Louis and was a journeyman printer on the *St. Louis Enquirer* under Thomas Hart Benton and Isaac N. Henry. He thereafter edited nine Missouri newspapers, all failures. His fellow editor Patten exclaimed, "Poor Keemle!" when he heard of plans for the suspension of the *St. Louis Beacon*, the official Jackson paper of that day. All of Keemle's papers, commented Patten, "have successively descended to the 'tomb of the Capulets,'" and so would his future enterprises go to the grave, where reposed his other numerous progeny.[33] Patten's prophecy successfully prefigured Keemle's career. His last newspaper and also his last failure was the *Weekly Reveille*, with Matthew and Joseph Field, probably the most important literary journal before the Civil War. But it had no greater success than his other journals.

Despite Keemle's failure as a newspaper editor, his Book and Job Printing Office was a prosperous concern — its gazetteers, counting-house calendars, and directories were well received — and he rose to a position of pre-eminence in social and political affairs of St. Louis. Promoter of theater, dancing club, literary and debating society, and a racing enthusiast, he also held political office, although after he had crossed from the Jacksonian to the Whig party, he refused political favors from Presidents Harrison and Taylor.[34]

A kind of itinerancy in reverse resulted when a newspaper had a frequent succession of editors. No newspaper had such an array of editors — nor such a succession of mastheads — as the *Western Journal* — *The Emigrant and General Advertiser* — *St. Louis Enquirer* — *Missouri Advocate and St. Louis Enquirer.* Throughout its variegated career, it remained much the same newspaper, but its series of unsuccessful editors brought great comfort to its rival, the *Missouri Gazette* — *Missouri Republican.* Joseph Charless early cued the checkered history of the newspaper when he referred to its second editor, Sergeant Hall, as the "itinerant printer." He took up the charge again when Benton edited the paper, boasting that he had foretold the flight of Joshua Norvell and Sergeant Hall to Arkansas, and was now predicting Benton's retreat from "the magnificent valley of the Mississippi" — a Bentonian phrase — to South America. In this he was wrong, for Benton went to the Senate instead, but the succession of editors continued at an even faster rate than before. The *Republican* listed them. After Isaac N. Henry and Company (alias Benton and Company) came Patrick H. Ford; then Ford and Orr; Ford and Stine; Green and Ford; Duff Green; Foreman and Keemle; Foreman and Birch; Foreman; Birch.[35] With this, ended the history of a newspaper, although it did not end the efforts of the Jacksonian politicians to establish a newspaper.

IV

Sensing their lack of status, dissatisfied with their condition, editors complained that they were a beleaguered and bedeviled lot. The labor of editing and printing a paper, the perfidy of subscribers, the treachery of blackguard rivals and traitorous friends, an irregular mail, and the difficulty of securing proper materials led the editors to the conclusion that they were an abused race of beings. When Charles and Patten reminisced, usually at the beginning of each new volume, they remembered the frontier conditions and the hardships of establishing a press in the territorial period.

But they also vividly remembered the plots of unprincipled rivals who sought to starve out the honest, hardworking printer, treating him with arrogance or violence, persecuting him. The editor, unlike the soldier, the mechanic, or the merchant, was a sentinel who must never sleep. His toil was the toil of the brain, and his recompense — penury.[36] Procuring subscribers in the western country was an ungracious task, and the editor must have the patience of Job to meet the frivolous objections of would-be subscribers, who pleaded lack of time, poverty, hard times, or an inaccessible residence as reasons for not taking out a subscription.[37]

Upon assuming sole editorship of the *Jefferson Inquirer*, William Lusk commented on the duties, responsibilities, and difficulties under which the editor labored, but which were not generally understood by the populace. Before undertaking to publish a paper, the editor must have adequate resources to tide him over if his subscribers did not pay, since in all likelihood they would not. He must decide if he would edit a political or a neutral paper. If neutral, he would deny himself the privilege of expressing himself as a freeman, and would run the danger of reflecting, inadvertently, on a political party, in which case politicians and nine-tenths of the female readers would come down on him like an earthquake. If it was a political paper, there was the question of whether to be a purist or

moderate. If the former, moderate politicians would charge him
with being overbearing. If he was lukewarm, then "Dam your
half coon skin." Not the least of the editor's worries was the
sponger who managed to read the newspapers without sub-
scribing. He might be a close friend, who came into the office
to see just one paper, thinking he might subscribe. Or he might
ask to see an advertisement, or insert an advertisement and ask
to have the paper with the notice sent to him. If an advertiser
asked the charge, and was told the rate by squares, he might
reply, "Dam your squares — I'll not give you more than $1 —
money's too scarce." Thus toiled a beleaguered editor, who concluded he must take his own course and not try to please everybody.[38]

V

He could not please everybody, because his patrons thought
of him too often as a printer — on the same level as a mechanic
or artisan. True enough, many an editor labored away in the
print shop — too poor to hire journeymen or too backward to
progress with the times. Format, display, original matter —
evidences of editorial technique — held little favor among the
editorial brethren, although with the close of the pioneer period
these factors played an increasing role. Thus every editor was
concerned with the improvement of the mechanics and dress
of his enterprise, with a "neat and spicy sheet" and "respectability of appearance."[39] To them, progress was made on the craft
level and not on the editorial level. Theirs was an external, not
an internal theory of progress.

Every editor was aware that he should expand and improve
his facilities. All did so except perhaps Calvin Gunn, who remained "content to be among the poor."[40] Repeatedly, editors
strove to increase the size of their papers and to buy new type
and press. To do this, subscribers must pay up old bills, and
new patrons must be secured. In his first number of volume
eighteen, Patten called attention to the new type, which improved the external appearance of his paper, and expressed his

desire to procure soon a larger press if additional patronage permitted. To Patten this kind of improvement — the securing of better printing materials — should have aroused the pride of the liberal and enterprising citizens of Boone County much more than progress in editorial technique.[41] Charless printed the first issues of the *Gazette* on foolscap, but quickly set about to improve the paper which he fed into his press.[42] His eagerness for progress overreached itself once when he placed a very flowery and ornate masthead above the printed matter, so barely readable that Sergeant Hall lampooned it as the "Hieroglyphics at the head of the Gazette." [43]

VI

Failure to band together in the interest of dignity and profits cost so much public esteem that pioneer journalism came into disrepute. An *esprit de corps* was needed to bind journalists together into harmonious community, and it was to this task of professionalization that a number of editors devoted a great deal of earnest consideration.

The first signs of true professionalization came with the first editors' convention, in Missouri in 1859, from which developed eventually the Missouri Press Association. Calls for such a convention had been made at a very early date. Abel Rathbone Corbin of the *Missouri Argus* was not the first to propose a meeting when, in 1837, he suggested that editors and publishers of papers and masters of job offices from Illinois, Missouri, and Wisconsin meet in St. Louis to restore harmony among the group, for, as he put it, "we have been clawing each other's eyes out quite long enough." [44] Again, in 1839, the *Argus* proposed a convention of proprietors in St. Louis to adopt regulations and secure their enforcement against delinquent subscribers.[45] This meeting, however, did not come off, and the *Argus*, convinced that a convention of printers and publishers of the state was impossible, determined to go it "solitary and alone" to eliminate the credit system. The press of the whole country

was kept poor, dependent, and contemptible, because publishers were too liberal and accommodating to their friends.[46]

Throughout the 1840's futile efforts to bring together a state-
wide convention continued. William F. Switzler of the *Missouri
Statesman*, pointed to the benefits of the uniform tariff established by the members of the St. Louis press. He and F. M.
Caldwell of the *Boonville Observer* especially desired agree-
ments on advertising rates, which, though they appeared equa-
ble throughout the state, varied with every office because the
printer took anything he could get. A recognized tariff of prices
would be of great benefit to the craft and would raise the
editor — "emaciated from incessant toil . . . out at elbows and
out of money!" — from his low status in society.[47]

In 1853 a regional meeting of editors did take place in Savan-
nah. Lucian J. Eastin of the *St. Joseph Gazette* was made chair-
man, and James A. Millan of the *St. Joseph Cycle* was appointed
secretary. William Ridenbaugh, also of the *Gazette*, made an
address in which he spoke of the "Profession of Printing" as the
"noblest profession," but one that was left like the "weed cast
from the rock, on ocean's foam to float where e'er the waves
might roll or the winds prevail." The solution to the problem of
competitive prices, as in the other professions, was to unite to
protect themselves from ruinous competition. A date — the
second Monday in October — and a place — St. Louis — were
chosen for an editors' convention, to fix rates for printing.[48]

Nothing came of this, but the next year, 1854, new proposals
were made for a state editors' convention, which like all other
attempts proved abortive. The *Hannibal Journal* made suggestions for a meeting place — Hannibal, Boonville, Glasgow, or
some other point of easy access — but A. W. Simpson, recogniz-
ing the wisdom of the "craft" adopting uniform measures,
thought the only place where general attendance was possible
was St. Louis.[49] He noted that in the newspaper business the
overweening idea had been to get a circulation, and consequently subscriptions had been reduced to as low as one dollar

a year, while costs had advanced 10 to 20 per cent. Under these conditions no publisher could make a living, no matter how large the circulation. Whatever was circulated, circulated for glory.

Switzler also believed that all publishers had to do to raise their status was to band together, and like Simpson, saw a convention as a means of improving camaraderie. Serious efforts had been made to meet during the state fairs in Boonville, in 1853 and 1854, and in the latter year a few editors made their appearance. But the convention of 1854 failed because attendance was too small. While valuable suggestions were interchanged, the editors had no hope of adopting any resolutions which would win general acceptance. Those loudest in advocating a convention, complained Switzler, remained at home, and he was so discouraged that he regarded the subject as dead and buried for years to come.[50]

But his discouragement was premature. A successful convention finally met in Jefferson City, in 1859, under the aegis of Switzler. The editor of the *Louisiana Herald* announced he would be there and urged other editors to attend by asking them how long they intended to be slaves of quack doctors, one-horse politicians, and non-paying subscribers. The country printers, he asserted, knew they were doing wrong in publishing long columns of quack nostrums at starvation prices, or too frequently for no price at all, and lawyer-editors too often made themselves pack-horses of the shallow-pated orator. In a vein of humor he drew up an agenda in the form of an interrogatory:

> Fellow countrymen, did you ever know
> 1. a prompt-paying patent pill peddlar?
> 2. an honest Eastern advertising agent?
> 3. a menagerie man without mutilated money?
> 4. an office seeker that wouldn't lie? [51]

A sufficient number of editors in the state met on June 8, 1859, elected Switzler their first president, and drew up an effectual code of ethics and business operations.[52] This statement of intention marked a concerted attack on a number of features of pioneer journalism — ruthless competition, an emphasis upon the principles of the printing craft, lack of professional standards, a large concern for politics, and use of abusive language.

Moderation, fairness, dignity, courtesy — these were the virtues which would bring honor to the profession and restore the reputation of the press. And the punishment for the transgressor who disregarded these virtues? Censure by the other members of the profession, and for the repeated violator, forfeiture of the usual courtesies of the pen.

Twenty years earlier such a code, postulating moderation and courtesy, would have been impossible, for then the virtues were firmness, manliness, independence, an obligation to speak out bluntly on all the issues. An editor regarded his fellow editor with no particular courtesy; indeed, any wrongheaded ideas of one editor must be combated with impunity, for how else could truth be established against error of opinion. Now, in 1859, members of the press were mellowing. Manliness was giving way to moderation. *Esprit de corps* was replacing ruthless competition, the craft was giving way to the profession. The Missouri press fraternity now wanted status, to get status they needed respectability, and to be respectable they must be courteous.

To rise up from the "degradation of the press," the editors needed an agreement that they would not undercut one another's prices. So their code contained a set of business regulations which struck at the competition, the ruthless competition which had caused poverty for most and profits for only a few. After addressing itself rather briefly to courtesy and moderation, the Convention devoted the largest part of its statement to the matter of profits. Out-of-county subscribers and transient advertisers must pay in advance; book and job work must be paid for on delivery; yearly advertisers must settle their accounts periodically; patent medicine and lottery advertisements must be paid for in advance or guaranteed by a responsible local agent. The square, the unit of measurement for paid insertions in the newspaper, was defined so that it would contain no more nor no less than in any newspaper in the state. Furthermore, legal advertisements, a very lucrative form of advertisement, were to be paid for by the square. To further discourage credit, a 10 per cent interest would be charged on all accounts overdue.

Thus the Missouri Editors' Convention of 1859 attempted to change the course of pioneer journalism, seeking to end the time of roughness and crudeness and of loose financial methods, and to bring professional status to a beleaguered and meager occupation. But it was the fate of this organization to suffer from the depredations of the Civil War. The war brought great tribulation to the Missouri press, and it was not until normal times returned that progress toward professionalization could continue.

IV FARE FOR THE READER

CHAPTER 9

NEWS FOREIGN AND DOMESTIC

$\mathcal{N}$ATHANIEL PATTEN at one time carried underneath his masthead the motto, "Devoted to the defence of *Republican Principles* — to the support of *Agriculture, Commerce* and *Manufactures* — and to *Religious, Literary* and *Miscellaneous* subjects." This signified a wide range of interests for only twenty columns.[1] His successor, F. A. Hamilton of the renamed *Columbia Patriot*, gave the subscribers a preview of what he would put before them:

> News, foreign and domestic — whatever may be interesting in the proceedings of Congress and the State Legislatures — improvements and discoveries in the arts and sciences — facilities and successful experiments in husbandry and agriculture — the gems of poetry and beauties of belles-lettres — extracts from modern travels and from the daily works of the cotemporary [*sic*] press, shall all find a place in the columns of the Patriot: — particularly after materials can be had for its enlargement.[2]

As Patten's motto and Hamilton's announcement show, the concept of news embraced in broad compass — too broad — such
subject matter as would beguile every reader-interest group.

I

The pioneer editor had a conception of news which differed
from that of the twentieth century. He conceived of news as
belles-lettres, as novelty, as politics, and as idea.

Both Charless and Patten defined news as the "passing tidings
of the times."[3] Lacking objectivity, free of the inanities of
modern journalese, news thus had in it the elements of prose
and poetry. News to the pioneer editor was also literature;
he made efforts at grace in his own style, and printed articles
from the field of *belles-lettres*. He sought to include in his paper
the productions of local authors, who used the newspaper as a
vehicle for their self-expression, and he clipped from the eastern journals works which appealed to the tastes of the public.

Besides the idea of tidings, news also connoted novelty, or
new things. Webster, in the 1830 edition of his *Dictionary*, defined news as "fresh or novel accounts of events."[4] In order to
enhance the newsworthiness of an item, it had to be sensational.
To prospective patrons who would become subscribers, Patten
promised

> to communicate the earliest notice of all wars, pestilence,
> famine and earthquakes — and what is of infinite greater
> importance, an early account of every open conspiracy
> against the constitution, and Union of the States.[5]

In addition to the belletristic and the bizarre, events of political nature were considered newsworthy. In the eighteenth century a politician and editor formed an alliance, a fact noted by
Dr. Samuel Miller in his *Retrospect of the Eighteenth Century*.[6]
In Missouri journalism, newspapers were often founded, and
sometimes failed, in the cause of politics. Journals and laws of
the state and national governments, effusive orations from the
halls of the legislatures or the stump all found their way into

the pioneer newspaper. Nor did the editor flinch from political controversy, and this was the current which aroused him from his lethargy and galvanized his pen into original production. Nathaniel Patten, for instance, even though he hated the subject, devoted nearly half his 699 editorials to politics, writing more in the great election year of 1828 than in any other.[7]

Finally, the editor conceived of his news as idea, and included essays of political, religious, moral, agricultural, and scientific significance.[8] Joseph Charless gave his readers a clue as to the kind of news he would put into his columns. He desired

> Essays on Morals and government, concise pieces on history, (particularly the early settlement and progressive growth of Louisiana,) Antiquities, Topography, Botony [*sic*] and vegetable Materia Medica, and Mineralogy, with such hints on Husbandry as may tend to induce the planter to embrace those wonderful advantages nature has thrown in his way, Indian manners and customs with their best speeches, Cases argued and determined in our Courts, or any thing that may contribute to enliven the passing moment by an ingenious Tale or Song, [which] will be gratefully received and carefully inserted.[9]

But news communicated as idea came not on a high intellectual level. It had to be understandable to a heterogeneous population, widely scattered, and little schooled. It had to be unsubtle and easy to comprehend.

The editors themselves did not characterize their news as *belles-lettres*, as novelty, as politics, as idea, but they did place their own stipulations on their news. News must be useful, entertaining, interesting, informative, moderate, beneficial to the public, diverse in subject matter and origin, of a public and not a private nature, and it must be on a foundation of principles. Tubal E. Strange announced that he would "use his best endeavors to publish a useful and beneficial paper." Stephen W. Foreman and Robert M'Cloud in their prospectus for the St. Charles *Missouri Gazette* promised "to gratify, to serve, and to instruct the public." Editors avowed a belief in the sanctity of private character, but public men and measures were fit subjects for "animadversion and approbation." [10]

Since the pioneer journal resembled more a general magazine than a newspaper in content, the editor had to compress into a four-page folio sheet the greatest variety of material. Consequently, most subscribers expressed dissatisfaction with him, because he slighted the one department which they most liked to read. Nathaniel Patten illustrated with a reprint the woes of a beleaguered editor victimized by the shafts of these "Grumbletonians." Mr. Thunderbolt wanted more battles, murders, convulsions, floods, famines, fires, pestilence, shipwrecks, storms, and tempests. Mr. Thoughtful favored more news of a peaceable and pleasant nature, of times gone by, the progress of truth, the suppression of slavery, the civilization of the Indians, and the conversion of the heathen. Miss Flutterbudget desired conundrums, acrostics, anecdotes, epigrams, poetry, light miscellany, love adventures, and marriages. Mr. Political Plain Truth wanted columns of Presidential messages, Congressional debates, public documents, and governors' speeches. Doctor Pepper Pot wanted more political sharp shooting and electioneering; he demanded:

> Give us more of the real essence, the genuine Cayenne pepper of political sharp shooting — with now and then an emetic of the real lobelia of electioneering, that will set the whole body politic to vomiting, and raise the political steam-engine to such a pressure, as will throw the camp of the enemy into utter confusion, out of mere terror at *letting off* the steam!

Mr. Newsmonger wanted more of the Greeks and South American Patriots. Mrs. Ellen Etymology desired more physiognomy, hornithology, *had-u*-cation, and poets of antiquity, to prepare her to put her boys through college "and have 'em *come out* bright as a pewter spoon." Mr. Yorrick Yardstick demanded more commercial intelligence. Mr. Moses Mechanic wanted more notices of new inventions, a dissertation on the utility of patent pumps, pea-straw hats, and wooden nutmegs, or some other labor-saving machine. Mr. Oliver Ox Bow, the farmer who sat quietly listening to the complaints and arguments of the Grumbletonians, finally said that the editor could not please everybody, and counseled him to manage his own concerns in his own way. But he should not forget to publish the farmer's department. Mr. Ox Bow's closing advice to the editor, which Patten intended as the message of the piece, was above all to print the truth.[11]

II

Newspapers in the early nineteenth century remained so much in their infancy that they still reflected the original purpose for which they had come into being — the conveyance of foreign news. The first newspapers in England brought intelligence of the Thirty Years' War, and throughout the seventeenth and eighteenth centuries the emphasis continued to fall on foreign accounts.[12] By far the greatest amount of space in the pioneer papers was taken up with two subjects: foreign news and the public printing.

During his first seven years, probably no figure captured the attention of Editor Charless as much as Napoleon. Evidently, his readers queried him on what would happen after the exile of the Emperor to Saint Helena.

> *A candid Reply to a common Question.*
> We are often asked, "Now Bonaparte is imprisoned, and the world at peace, what will you fill your papers with?"
> We answer — we shall fill it
> With the laws of the United States & of this territory, which it is the interest and duty of every citizen to understand and obey —
> With the Proceedings and Votes of our national and territorial Legislature on questions of general importance — of which no politician ought to be ignorant, if he estimates his right of suffrage at its true value and desires so to exercise it that it may operate "as a terror to evil-doers, and a praise to them that do well" —

With the acts and appointments of our federal and local executives, of which all must have a curiosity to be informed —

With the correspondence between our own and foreign governments on questions arising out of our commercial and political intercourse with them —

With essays and observations on the provisions of our constitutions, and the measures of our administrations, and in favor of the principles of independence, Liberty and Union —

With the projects and enterprizes of Authorities, Associations, and Individuals, to develope & augment the wealth, strength, respectability and happiness of our country —

With accounts of the improvements in agriculture — progress in Manufactures — prosperity of Commerce — inventions [in] the Arts — and discoveries in the sciences —

With the Results of Elections, and other interesting Domestic Occurrences —

With the heads of all important Foreign Transactions.

With religious, Political, Medical, Legal & Literary intelligence.

With Historical, Biographical and Geographical sketches —

With Poetry; Anecdotes — Wit and Humor —

With Births (when more than two at once) and Deaths — with Marriages and Elopements —

And last (tho' not the least advantageous to us, nor the least useful to the community) Advertisements; by which buyers learn where to find the houses, farms, merchandize or other articles, they want, and sellers obtain more customers and better prices, &c. &c. &c.[13]

Charless, the Irish rebel of 1795, derived his interest in Napoleon from his overweening Anglophobia. Events abroad especially interested him and his fellow editors if they portended the establishment of freedom and liberty on the American model. When the Neapolitans and Spanish revolted in 1820, the Greeks in 1821, the Canadians in 1837, the Latin Americans in the second decade, the editors presented to the reading public the case of the revolutionaries, through reprints from the eastern journals. The exploits of the heroes and liberators who struck a blow for freedom always earned the interest of the American reading public, who looked with pride upon the emulation of their own republic. But, in this as in all matters, editors excerpted copy from the eastern and foreign journals and composed little that was original to their columns.

III

But one bit of news, conspicuous by its absence, did not meet the eye of the gentle reader. The earliest editions of papers edited by Joseph Charless, Thomas H. Benton, Nathaniel Patten, Tubal E. Strange, and Stephen Remington contained little local news. Evidently, intelligence of the community circulated by word of mouth, and the editor felt no need either to accept communications from local authors about local events, or to seek information himself immediately beyond his doorstep. Occasionally, the death or marriage of a prominent personage was noted in the journal, and perhaps a passing reference was made to an economic or social event of the locality. But a chronicle of local history was not believed newsworthy. Even "domestic news" denoted state and national politics, and not community and county activities.

The first signs of the localizing of the press begin to appear in the pioneer period, culminating in a great revolution after the Civil War. Over the years the amount of local news increased to some extent, so that by 1861 it could be measured in tens of thousands of column inches, rather than mere hundreds.[14] Speaking before the Missouri Press Association in 1876, William F. Switzler noted that Missouri journalism had become completely revolutionized by the introduction of the telegraph and the transportation of mails by railroad, which had largely localized the county press. Later in life, Switzler said that no paper had a local department until 1858, although he could have mentioned that the *Missouri Republican* had one as early as 1837, a time when the city press of St. Louis was beginning to take giant strides away from pioneer journalism.[15]

Before the revolution, local news was placed in the editorial section. There it competed with political comments and exhortations, and as a result fared badly. At first the printer devoted little space to the editorial. With little or no comment he often printed documents, such as constitutions, legislative proceedings, laws, long-winded speeches, and the minutes of meetings, leaving the reader to draw his own conclusions.

In presenting the political, editors often incidentally and imperfectly revealed glimpses into the local news of the community. Patten gives us a tantalizing glance into the stripping of the Birch faction of its authority in Fayette in 1833,[16] but the full story of what happened will have to be reconstructed from other sources. The most domestic news was state politics, which filled the pages of the newspaper, while the remoteness of an event seemed to increase its importance. As Franklin W. Scott said about Illinois newspapers, there seemed to be more interest in the hop yield in Silesia than in the wheat crop in Illinois.[17]

IV

Occasionally the editor had to apologize for dearth of news, which resulted from a failure of the mails, a lack of time, or an absence of what the editor considered news. The following was a common, almost a weekly complaint with the pioneer editor:

> We are unable this week to present our readers with anything new or particularly interesting; the failure of the mail for the last two weeks, has left us almost without resource, and we are compelled to make up our columns with such matter as circumstances have left attainable.[18]

Then, finally, the mail would arrive, and with it a half bushel of newspapers: four *Niles Weekly Register's*, five *New York American's*, nine *Washington Republican's*, twenty-five *National Intelligencer's*, but all at least thirty-four days from the press, and some nearly twice that old.[19] The editor of the *Missouri Repub-*

lican, like his brethren, filled up space with lamentations over the dearth of news. He contended it was not his fault if the political ocean was calm. "We cannot make Bonapartes. . . . Nor can we compel the Holy Alliance to make war on the liberties of Europe." Furthermore, state and national affairs were calm. "As to the whole tribe of 'melancholy accidents,' 'horrid murders,' 'awful catastrophes,' " etc., they had become vulgar by being too common. The *Republican* editor thought that, at least, something probably would transpire by the fourth of March next.[20]

But occasionally the editor admitted there was a dearth of news because he had lacked time to compose it before going to the press.[21] And he often crowded out news for other reasons, too. A presidential or gubernatorial inaugural, a new constitution, the journals of the national and state legislatures, the speech of a statesman, or the proceedings of county party conventions could well crowd out other information to which readers had become accustomed. The state printer often could not maintain his regular services during the busy season when the legislature convened. Calvin Gunn printed only a bare half sheet while he was engaged in compiling and publishing the legislative journals.[22] An increase in the demand for job work sometimes made inroads upon the newspaper enterprise.[23]

When an editor moved to a new office or even to a new town, a diminution, even a temporary suspension, of activities might be necessary. Patten missed only one number when he moved from Franklin to Fayette.[24] A failure in the supply of paper, due to inadequate transportation facilities, might force the editor to print on a smaller sheet of inferior quality.[25] Labor problems, such as illness among the workmen or shorthandedness, might cause a curtailment.[26] During a cholera epidemic, no edition of the Palmyra *Missouri Courier* appeared for at least two weeks.[27] Patten reduced his paper to one-half sheet when his wife died.[28]

V

As a literary stylist, the pioneer editor wrote in the Romantic tradition, although he attempted to imitate the forms of classical scholars. In effect, he tried pouring new wine into old bottles, the new wine having the sweet aroma of the Reverend Laurence Sterne, and the bottles labeled Addison and Steele, Pope, or Dryden.[29] But the literary character of a frontier newspaper was not determined entirely by the style of the editor. Much of the printed matter was contributed by local men of letters or reprinted from other journals.

The editor and his correspondents wrote in an unrestrained manner, with frequent reliance upon the superlative, often indicated by the use of italics. The language often became abusive, so abusive that violence resulted. Besides the superlative, newspaper authors also used the satiric pun, in an attempt to wound and discomfit their opponents. Thus the *Jefferson Inquirer* styled the Jefferson City *Metropolitan* as the "Littlepolitan."[30] Nathaniel Patten paid his old enemy, James H. Birch, who for a time was Secretary of the State Senate, the dubious compliment of "Mr. Scratchetary Birch," and once called his *Western Monitor* the "*Western Monster.*"[31] One of Joseph Charless' correspondents characterized Editor Thomas H. Benton of the *St. Louis Enquirer* as "The Enquirer-man, bent-on mischief."[32] Of a dancing master who failed to pay his newspaper bill, the *Missouri Republican* punned, "It therefore became necessary for him to take some *step*, and true to his vocation, he *chasse'd* up the river, . . ."[33]

In the pioneer papers many Missourians read, for the first time, Major Jack Downing, Washington Irving, James Fenimore Cooper, or Walter Scott. The experiences of frontiersmen such as Mike Shuck and Hugh Glass were transcribed with the flavor of the tall tale into prose by Missouri's most famous frontier author, Alphonso Wetmore. Among poets, Byron was a favorite, but many minor poets were popular, partly because their sketches were short and more suitable to a small paper. In prose, the editor selected humorous essays, while in poetry, love, marriage, and death (but not birth) were popular subjects. Religion found relatively little place in the columns of the newspaper, since the editors wished to avoid religious controversy. Like the authors of political pieces, contributors of literary compositions also used pseudonyms, such as "Aurora Borealis," "T," and "Lucy's Cousin."[34]

Every newspaper had a poetry corner to which local bards contributed their rhyme and in which editors placed reprints from other journals. Poems were in tone didactic, elegiac, eulogistic, and in the case of political compositions, invective.[35] An annual custom in the journalism world was the carriers' address, delivered on the first day of each year to the doors of the subscribers. These addresses usually began with a review of the year's events and somewhere contained an encomium on the great "republic of the West." The lighthearted humor is illustrated in the following quotation from the *Missouri Intelligencer*. After mentioning the workaday world in several lines, the carrier boy continues:

> But themes like this [the workaday world] a carrier boy
>   should shun,
> And, the news once spread, conceive his labor done;
> Save when a year slips through his finger ends,
> Then he may make review, to make amends
> In his lean heritage — his weekly *range*
> May yield him some few *vagrant bits* of change.
> Since, then, the annals of the year begun,
> Much have *you* read — much more the *boy* has run. . . .
>
> Patrons, *we*'ve done! — if what *we*'ve said be sense,
> Your fingers fob, to fish up *eighteen pence*![36]

VI

That the pioneer editor assumed the functions of a true editor only with reluctance is further illustrated by the general make-up of his newspaper. In the matter of headline, illustration, and format, and in the matter of advertising, the editor made few innovations over the years. He seldom used imagination to stimulate reader interest or to make his page more attractive.

If he used a headline, and often he did not, it was the label-type headline, which gave little clue as to the news content below it. It might simply be "Agriculture," "Medical," "Legislature," or "Important!" "Horrid Accident!" and "War!! War!!" The paragraph sign, the index hand, and the section mark did yeoman service in supplanting the headline. The early headlines often expressed merely emotion. The single crossline heading, without a verb, was nearly always used; and a double line or more, indented in any way, was unknown. Mechanically, it was possible to develop a headline which would attract the interested reader, and which would give some indication of news content, but the editor did not lead the way; rather, he allowed social pressures to force new developments in the use of the headline. Wars and political contests brought some innovations in headline technique, but the tendency was to revert to the old style after the special events were over. The Mexican War lessened the editor's conservatism only temporarily.[37]

Editors did not often use illustrations, and those used were chiefly in advertisements. The earliest illustrations were woodcuts, and since they appeared time and again, were blurred by wear. Metal cuts were apparently used and type foundries advertised stereotyping, which was probably for illustrative purposes.[38] One of the earliest illustrations was a finely cut patriotic emblem, which appeared above the Laws of the United States. The number of illustrations increased on the eve of the Civil War, but the editor thought nothing of imposing the same picture upon his readers for an interminable period.

The format of the newspaper also lacked imagination and originality, again because the journalist had not completely separated the functions of an editor from those of a practical printer. While he strove to execute his paper neatly and in a workmanlike manner, the aim of the printer-craftsman, he did not have any conception of the arts of display and of make-up, which are the concerns of the editor. Indeed, his was an amorphous page, with little variation in the solidly packed printed columns.

Advertising constituted a considerable part of the contents of pioneer newspapers, and, in some cases filled more than half an issue. Tocqueville commented on the great distinction between American and French journals — the devotion of as much as three-fourths of the American paper to advertisements, as compared to the nearly exclusive concern of the French periodical for passionate political discussion.[39] From a professional standpoint, these advertisements had little to commend them, yet in many ways they offer better clues to the local history of the times than the news and editorial sections.

The advertisements, like all other elements of the pioneer newspaper, showed a lack of editorial talent, in that they were bare announcements which informed the public in a simple, unadorned, factual way of goods or services for sale. Headlines were rarely selective, unless they read "To the Ladies," or "To Farmers and Mechanics." Usually they merely said "Look," "Notice," "Just Received," "The Subscriber," or "Tavernkeeping." Because the type was crowded close together, leaving little if any white space, the advertising columns gave the dull, monotonous appearance of the want-ad sections of today. The editor used little imagination in arranging his advertisements. It was not until the 1830's that some editors began grouping their public announcements into categories — legal, stray, general store, etc. Although no page was free from the notices, they tended to be concentrated on the first and fourth pages. Rarely more than a column wide, the editor gave no exclusive section to his advertisers. Neither first insertion on first page, nor last on fourth page, was considered superior.[40]

No matter how untimely an advertisement had become, it often greeted its readers, in issue after issue, with absolutely no change in format, display, or wording. This saved typesetting for the journeyman in the printing shop. Since the merchant purchased goods only once or twice a year, he felt little need to change the wording of an announcement. Then, too, it was cheaper for the advertiser to run his announcement for a long period of time, the price being reduced to as much as one-third after one month. There is evidence editors frequently allowed advertisements to remain in their columns after the advertiser no longer desired its appearance. These "dead advertisements" remained in the paper as filler, or because the editor hoped to force his patron to pay, by building up his bill. Also, it might remain there due to the slovenly business methods of the editor, or to a misunderstanding between editor and advertiser. In any case, the repetition of advertisements only increased the monotony of the already wearisome pages.[41]

Not all merchants recognized the value of advertising. The merchant might not advertise in a paper simply because he objected to the politics of its editor. Nor did the editor conceive of the advertising function as his primary purpose. For the twin reasons, then, of editorial and mercantile apathy, only about one-third of the merchants of a community used a newspaper as a sales promotion medium.[42]

No attempt was made to stimulate the desire of the reader for goods by captivating descriptions. No trade names, for the most part, were used. Nor did the merchant attract customers by a quotation of prices. Instead he fawned before his potential customers, always "flattering himself," "hoping to be of service," or "wishing respectfully to announce." The tone of the copy was deadly dull; indeed, both merchant and editor were content with a simple statement of fact, even if it became outdated.[43]

The editor and his advertiser did not forever remain backward in their advertising policy. In time, more imagination went into the make-up of an advertisement. Devices to attract attention began to be used, such as the use of display type, the setting of type to conform to designs like a diamond or a wine glass, and, if the imagination was less fertile, placing the advertisement sideways or upside down in the column. The merchant came to realize the value of white space, and allowed the editor to indent and skip a line so that the advertisement was not crammed with print. Some enterprising merchants adopted slogans, the most common of which was "I am determined to sell lower than any other house in the United States." Illustrations, symbolic of the ware advertised, captured the attention of the reader and suggested to him the content of the advertisement below.[44]

At first, editors had available for illustration a small hand with index finger pointing, which they used profusely, in an attempt to give some distinction to an advertisement. Also, in this early period, they occasionally employed what probably were woodcuts. Charless first used a small cut of several boots and shoes for a shoemaker's advertisement, and then, several years later, an emblem with the words "Approved Family Medicines" for a patent medicine notice, a house in a setting for notices of farms and lots for sale, and a small horse with a boy for stray advertisements. One of the first large illustrations was a distilling flask with downward spout and condensing coil, used in a copper- and tin-smith advertisement, which in time became quite worn and blurred.[45] Illustrations, however, did not long remain in such crude condition, as is evident in the papers prior to the Civil War, for by the end of the pioneer period type foundries furnished print shops with finely cut stereotype, which made illustrations of good quality.

As the development of advertising continued, the editor called the attention of his subscribers to particular advertisments in another part of the newspaper, especially if they were new. These editorial puffs indicate that the editor wanted advertising business.

The editor of the *Boonville Observer* in 1846, C. W. Todd, showed an increasing awareness of the value of advertising, when he appealed to businessmen under the caption "Philosophy of Advertising." He first pointed out to the merchants that people were more likely to come to a place if its name had become familiar to them by the frequent sight of it in the newspaper. This was especially true of subscribers in the country, who had no fixed place of purchase in town. But more important, continued Todd, was the impression that the reader of the paper had of the advertiser. By advertising he showed that he was anxious for business, and this sort of person was supposed to be industrious, civil, attentive, and desirous of pleasing customers. Moreover, those who advertised received more liberal patronage and could thus reduce prices, and the reader would know this. Editor Todd closed his appeal by disavowing motives of selfishness for desiring large amounts of advertising, because the editor found his own interest in laboring to promote the interest of all.[46]

Thus, advertisements in the pioneer journals showed no inclination to influence the buyer by the use of the superlative or by the creation of an idyllic image. No effort was made to induce quantity buying. Nor did these pioneer advertisements reflect the existence of any high degree of competition among businessmen. But a great revolution was taking place in one kind of advertising which was eventually to influence advertising as a whole. In patent medicine advertising, presenting the nostrums of the quack doctor to a gullible public, nearly every rule of pioneer advertising was broken, and modern-day methods were anticipated. Some of the patent medicine advertisements ran for several columns; they early used refined illustrations; they promised to cure anything by the use of the superlative; they created the idyllic image of perpetual health, with the device of the testimonial. Certainly one of the most important subjects to the nineteenth-century American was his health, and the patent medicine advertisements held out hope for the afflicted.[47] When Dr. Dyott announced his Celebrated Stomachic Elixir of Health or Dr. Fitch promised he could cure colds, coughs, consumption, asthma, heart disease, dyspepsia, scrofula, skin diseases, rheumatism, female complaints, piles, etc., the message was irresistible.[48]

Patent medicine advertising departed from pioneer methods also in the practice of national advertising. It was not uncommon for the country papers to carry St. Louis advertisements or the prospectuses of eastern newspapers or magazines, but they did not contain advertising of national products on a concerted scale, except for patent medicines. These notices were paid for by the eastern manufacturer.[49]

The editors filled their pages with useful, entertaining, and informative copy. Their news items satisfied the needs of a populace hungry for intelligence. Certain limitations existed, however, as the editors selected and published reading matter for their patrons. Their methods of news gathering affected the news itself, and we must turn now to the editors as reporters.

CHAPTER 10

PUBLICK PRINTS AND
PRIVATE LETTERS

𝒯HE METHODS of gathering news had improved little since the day Benjamin Franklin wrote in his *Pennsylvania Gazette* of October 23, 1729:

> The Publishers of this Paper meeting with considerable Encouragement, are determined to continue it; and to that End have taken Measures to settle a general Correspondence, and procure the best and earliest Intelligence from all Parts. We shall from time to time have all the noted Publick Prints from Great Britain, New-England, New-York, Maryland and Jamaica, besides what News may be collected from private letters and Informations; and we doubt not of continuing to give our Customers all the satisfaction they expect from a Performance of this Nature.[1]

Franklin and the Missouri pioneer editor alike utilized as the two main sources of news, reprints from other newspapers and communications from individuals — the "Publick Prints" and "private letters" Franklin had mentioned.

I

The pioneer editor owed a great debt to the newspaper work of his colleagues. Through a system of exchange he received the journals from the East as well as from the West. From them he clipped freely; his scissors and paste pot were in constant use. The editor's exchange list was large, and occasionally he declared his intention to cut his list down. The large exchange provided the editor with a voluminous news source, made possible by the privilege of free postage between publishers.

The pioneer editor would probably never have founded his journal, had Congress not established such favorable mail conditions for his benefit. Without the benefit of the free postage law of 1792, the editor could hardly have found enough copy to set to type. This law allowed free exchange between editors, and also to persons who enjoyed the franking privilege.[2] The Post Office Department frequently attempted to reduce the number of newspaper copies sent free, for the practice caused endless trouble. In 1822 the Department proposed to dispense with the privilege, and again, in 1825, to limit the exchange to fifty for each paper. These proposals excited such angry protests from the editors, whose privileges and very existence seemed threatened, that they failed of enactment.[3]

After the number of Missouri presses had increased sufficiently, Missouri editors began to reprint articles from each other, usually political pieces. The eastern journals supplied news of a more enduring character, where a time lag mattered little — articles on agricultural improvements, medicine, and sensational events such as personal catastrophes and natural phenomena, commercial and foreign news, political news of other states, and prose and poetry selections. Congressional news came from the files of Duff Green, Gales and Seaton, or Blair and Rives. If the editor was an official publisher of the laws of the United States, he got his material directly from the State Department. He extracted notices of the proceedings and the acts of the Missouri legislature from the newspaper of the official state printer, who sat as a reporter at the bar of the House or Senate.

II

The editor also relied for news upon the subscribers and interested parties who wrote on the subjects of politics and literature. If they discussed politics, they often sought to vindicate positions they had taken and which rivals had criticized. In so doing, they frequently employed language that led to violence. These contributions from subscribers rarely, if ever, discussed local events, but rather satisfied the yearning of some local would-be Sterne, Cooper, or Irving to enter the company of the literati, or of some aspiring Jefferson, Adams, or Clay to enter the circle of statesmen. As a rule, competition among newspapers increased the contributions. Before Charless and Patten had rivals in their respective towns, the populace seemed to be less articulate.

The authors of these contributions hid behind pseudonyms such as "Aristides," "A Gallo-American," "A Farmer," "Timothy Slash-em," or "A Friend to the Constitution," indicating, perhaps, the role which they intended to play. In any case, anonymity lent itself to virulence and contumely, so that the *nom de plume* became a *nom de guerre*. And this despite all the professions of moderation and openness by the editor. The possible repercussions from a vitriolic attack upon an opponent was feared much less if the attack was made under an assumed name. The early pioneer editors failed to spell out in detail their policy concerning anonymous contributions, and when they spelled it out, they did not live up to it. They announced that personal abuse and slander would not find a place in their columns, but they could hardly expect their contributors to live up to a rule which they themselves violated.

They would also announce that all contributors must enclose their real names with their letters, to be held for the time when afflicted parties should demand to know who had defamed them.

This requirement should have stemmed the tide of abuse, but since the editor himself engaged so ardently in the lists, he could not refuse to publish letters which were weapons to strengthen his own position, little matter how violent. The net effect was a lack of policy, and the editor himself had to bear the brunt when he published the inflammatory or untruthful communications of others. Charless unwisely refused to divulge the name of "Q" to injured persons, which led to a physical attack upon his person.[4] Once, when Patten uncritically accepted an item, he had to apologize to the brothers Birch, his mortal enemies in Fayette, for misinformation which it contained.[5] However, after several unfortunate experiences the editors adhered more to their resolutions not to admit completely anonymous articles, and absolutely refused to publish productions unless the name of the correspondent was enclosed.[6]

When an editor printed an item under an assumed name, it immediately excited speculation as to the real author. Sometimes the guessing was accurate, and sometimes not. When John B. C. Lucas, under the pen name "A Gallo-American" attacked the proposals of Stephen W. Foreman and Charles Keemle to begin a French language newspaper, these editors correctly inferred Lucas' authorship and began attacking him as the "old communications maker" and one of the "Whiskey Boys." They attempted to discredit him for whatever part he played in the Whiskey Rebellion in Pennsylvania. Whereupon Lucas discarded his pen name and counterattacked in the columns of the *Missouri Republican* and in a separate circular which he had printed. Since Foreman and Keemle edited the *Advocate*, the lineal descendant of Thomas Hart Benton's old paper, it was easy for Lucas to transfer his hatred for his son's killer to the two successors of Editor Benton.[7]

But the editors of the *Advocate* did not always correctly identify the authorship of communications in the *Missouri Republican*. The *Republican* smugly announced that the *Advocate* had been striking in the dark concerning some anti-Benton com-

munications, for the gentleman named by the *Advocate* was
not the author. The *Republican* took the position that it was
unimportant who wrote a communication, since neither the
truth nor fact depended upon a name, be it humble or magnificent.[8]

The use of the fictitious signature offered prominent politicians the opportunity to express themselves behind the cloak of
anonymity. Editors sometimes sought these expressions, so that
they actually became plants and not contributions. Indeed, it
was charged that journalists themselves wrote some of their
own letters to the editor, an allegation which R. H. Miller of
the *Liberty Tribune* denied for himself.[9]

Adam B. Chambers of the *Missouri Republican* solicited re-
joinders from George C. Sibley to the political presentments of
Thomas Hart Benton, writing in the *Missouri Argus*. He suggested that Sibley write under a name he had used before in
newspaper columns — "Solomon Salt." [10] Governor Daniel
Dunklin contributed to the *Missouri Argus* a number of articles,
two of which were signed "Democratus" and "Hampden."
"Democratus" favored a limitation on the tenure of justices of
the Supreme Court, and attacked Edward Bates and the *Missouri Republican*, under the assumption that these two parties
would never demand his real identity. "Hampden's" was an anti-
slavery tract. While Dunklin frequently assumed the position
of an authority in his articles, he disarmed his readers by referring to himself in rather distant terms.[11] At another time,
when the editor of the *Argus*, Abel Rathbone Corbin, was sick,
a little coterie of Jacksonian politicians filled the sheet with
pieces signed "A Miner," "A Citizen of Missouri," and "Jefferson." [12] These plants served a political purpose in a day when
partisanship had wrested control from impartiality.

When the first pioneer papers were founded in Missouri,
political parties had not yet fully developed, and editors were
more impartial in publishing communications from their
readers. The elder Charless, for instance, published articles on

both sides of the Missouri question in 1819. A few citizens, dissatisfied with the pro-restrictionist articles (although Charless himself opposed Congressional restrictions on the admission of a new state) and suspicious of Charless' anti-slavery views, demanded that these articles cease. When he refused, they stopped their subscriptions. This gave Charless an opportunity to trumpet the principle of liberty of the press, and to remind his readers of his slogan, "Truth without Fear." [13] Occasionally, Patten published the views of a subscriber which differed from his own, but he refused to print one upholding South Carolina in the nullification controversy. Any other doctrine but disunion he could countenance.[14]

After the rise of political parties, however, when newspapers became frankly the mouthpieces of factions, each gaining subscriptions only from people of one political persuasion, the journals became monolithic in the presentation of news. Each paper spoke as a political organ, not as a forum in which all sides participated. But communities had available more than one viewpoint since newspapers circulated widely, and nearly every community had access both to a Whig and a Democratic paper, if not of local origin, then by mail.

Nevertheless, despite the monolithic character of their papers, editors often attempted to restrain their anonymous correspondents who wrote with such fervor. The *Missouri Republican* vainly laid down a policy for its correspondents to follow. Announcing that the paper was open to all for a candid and fair discussion of issues, the editors at the same time stated that they could not accept anything of a personal nature. And they added that communications might also be refused if (1) the subject was exhausted, (2) it already had received a fair hearing, (3) it was inconvenient to prolong the controversy, (4) there were subjects of higher moment to the community which took precedence, or (5) the piece was not sufficiently condensed and methodical to serve the purpose for which it was intended.[15] These restrictions plus the stipulation that correspondents enclose their names, sums up the position of the most advanced editors on publishing communications, but still a journal as staid and conservative as the *Missouri Republican* was sued for libel.[16]

III

But the pioneer editors did not rely entirely upon other newspapers and letters to the editor as did Franklin. A great advance in reportorial technique occurred in the field of politics.

From the very beginning of Missouri journalism, the papers carried the journals of the Missouri legislature. These journals were, of course, bound and distributed to the public by authority of the legislature, but while the General Assembly was still in session, the reports were published in the newspapers. These reports were compiled by official reporters who were admitted to the halls of the House or Senate. Ordinarily, the official reporter presented himself by virtue of a contract which had been let by the legislature, but other reporters, who had no immediate pecuniary interest in the matter, also gained admittance. All of the Jefferson City papers, whether they had a contract or not, probably maintained reporters at one time or another.[17] While editors outside of the capital generally offprinted the proceedings of the legislature from the Jefferson City papers, it was not unknown for one of them to be admitted to the floor of the House or Senate. The Senate admitted to its halls W. F. Birch, editor of the *Western Monitor* of Fayette, although Birch did not at the time have the public printing.[18] In time many editors attended the legislature, if not to send home proceedings, at least to send back letters on the political maneuverings in the capital, and, if they had party influence, to direct these maneuvers as best they could.[19]

Politics, which had spurred the letter writer into print, stirred the editor himself into wielding the pen. The early editions of the pioneer newspapers — the *Missouri Gazette*, the *St. Louis Enquirer*, the *Independent Patriot*, and the *Missouri Intelligencer* — showed little evidence of the personality of the editor.

But politics and rivalry quickly changed all of that. Soon, on the second or third page, under a local dateline, appeared short commentaries by the editor, which he had composed just before going to press. Sometimes these evidences of editorial function consisted only of a few disconnected sentences or short paragraphs; at other times, they ran to half a column, and occasionally to one or two whole columns. The editor did not distinguish between what was news and what was his own opinion. He never hesitated to express his views at the very time he was reporting an event or calling attention to a selection in another part of the paper.

Readers soon came to expect the brief but tantalizing productions from the editor's pen. When the subscriber complained about the lack of originality, the editor either apologized or tried to justify his meager efforts. Frequently, the editor contributed nothing, because he was absent from the printing office. When James Lusk failed to return from St. Louis on the expected date, his underlings apologized for the lack of original matter in the newspaper which they put out.[20] The absence of editorial writing was more apt to occur if the editor was his own business manager as well as editor, rather than merely an editor, but the separation of editorial and proprietary duties often represented a stage beyond the frontier.

The editor could rationalize the existence of a barren and uninteresting sheet by pleading a dull and gloomy imagination, as F. M. Caldwell did in his *Boonville Observer*,[21] or by blaming the financial cares which weighed down an embarrassed and haggard editor, as J. C. Cummins did in his *Missouri Gazette*. How can it be expected that an editor will write anything orginal, protested Cummins, when he is constantly racking his brain for a way to pay for paper, ink, and workmen?[22]

IV

And yet as news gatherer, the pioneer editor had many limitations. He made little, if any, effort to go out after the news or to verify what he received. Common phrases which indicated his technique of news gathering were "we are informed," "we are authorized," "we are requested," "common report has it," and even "it is rumored." [23] Calvin Gunn described "rumor" as a fruitful source of news among some of his profession.[24]

In one of Charless' early issues, he falsely reported a French declaration of war against the United States in 1808 and was obliged to disavow it in the next edition. This inspired caution in him, when he noted, a few months later a rumor of an American declaration against both England and France, a report which he thought probable, but premature.[25] Editors James Lusk and S. L. Smith, ardent Democrats, in one of the most unusual political blurbs of the period, announced in a two-column, page-long advertisement, containing a cut of a great crowing rooster, that Pennsylvania had gone for the Democracy in 1840. But several issues later they noticed, not quite so flamboyantly, that the Keystone state had gone for Harrison by a 260-vote margin.[26] The editor could not even depend on articles from other journals which he reprinted, as the editors of the *Boonville Observer* discovered to their chagrin.

> The story about the murder of Miss Jackson at Russelville, Ky., in our last week's paper turns out to be a hoax which was perpetrated by some miscreant on the Louisville Journal.[27]

An editor often inferred events from knowledge which he had received, but which did not justify his conclusions. Two notable examples of this are the cases of H. M. Brackenridge and Governor Ninian Edwards, as reported in Joseph Charless' paper. After printing Brackenridge's essays, "Sketches of the Territory of Louisiana," Charless had incorrectly reported that the Pennsylvanian was going farther west to Mexico City, to gather material for a book. Brackenridge sent a demurrer to this report of Charless, who published a retraction in his paper.[28] In the case of Governor Edwards, Charless inferred, on incomplete evidence, that the Governor was guilty of disloyalty.

When Charless noted that Governor Edwards granted licenses to Indian traders who aided the British in the War of 1812, Edwards rejected the implication as a censure of him, and insisted he had not improperly granted the licenses. Charless, influenced by his rabid anti-British and anti-Indian bias, persisted in his charges, and Edwards later presented documents to Charless justifying his course. As a result, Charless had to exonerate Edwards of any culpability whatsoever.[29]

Because of his inadequate reporting methods, the editor stumbled in darkness when an important piece of news first broke. On the defalcation of the Treasurer of the state, Peter G. Glover, the *Liberty Tribune* reprinted from the *St. Louis Times*, which in turn had to be quite vague on all those implicated in the plot.[30]

In rare instances, an editor put off his editorial mantle and assumed the cloak of a reporter. The most frequent examples of this reporting are the descriptions of the thriving home towns and their great futures, of which the editors boasted to their readers.[31] But in these occasional and pseudo reportorial accounts, the editor did not have to leave his easy chair.

A slight advance in this reportorial technique occurred when Joseph Charless recalled a trip he had taken down the Ohio in 1795 by comparing civilization then with conditions in 1816.[32] But an even greater innovation, and unique for him, was the personal report Nathaniel Patten gave of his trip through Chariton County, describing the landscape of the county and the situations and prospects of the towns of Keytesville and Chariton.[33]

As long as local news remained in limbo, editors neglected the more advanced reporting techniques. The tendency toward local news, which began to creep into newspaper columns prior to 1860, was recognized occasionally in schemes to establish systems of regular local reporting. A. S. Mitchell conceived a plan wholly modern: to engage correspondents in every county, who once a week would write a letter to the newspaper containing a short history of deaths, fires, murders, markets, meetings, storms, earthquakes, elections, appointments, and arrests. "A complete week's history of Missouri!" he exclaimed. If such a plan could be extended beyond Missouri, Mitchell thought his newly founded St. Louis *Daily Evening News* might become the best newspaper in the world, but at that time his plan was too revolutionary for immediate acceptance.[34]

The pioneer editor, then, was not much of a reporter. He used other newspapers and letters to supply him with news. He began to make more personal exertions in the area of politics, and, to a much lesser degree, in the area of local news. The interview was yet unheard of. The whole character of news lacked a sense of timeliness, due, in part, to slow and irregular transportation, which made uncertain the reception of eastern news, but due, also to the editor's heavy involvement in the labors of the print shop, and in part to his own conservative frame of mind.

THE EDITOR AND THE FRONTIER

℃HE TRUE pioneer editor was the printer, who had risen through the ranks of apprentice and journeyman, and had performed all the functions of compositor (who set the type), impositor (who laid the set type on the stone and locked it up in the chase), pressman, editor, and business manager. As newspapers became more political in tone, the politician-editor, who devoted only part of his time to the enterprise, began to crowd the printer out, leaving him to superintend the print shop or to adjust as best he could to the new, politically dominated order. Indeed, in many cases where politics had become the underlying cause for a newspaper's existence, the words "editor" and "politician" seemed synonymous terms.

Unlike the lawyer, doctor, or preacher, the printer had no school of formal instruction to train him. His education took place in the printing office, under the apprentice and journeyman system. The first pioneers, of course, learned their trade in the East, or, as in the case of the Irish Charless, abroad. But in time Missouri began to train its own printers. Both the *Missouri*

Gazette and its successor, the *Missouri Republican*, educated many another pioneer editor in his craft. A smattering of the craft could also be learned from printers' assistants, textbooks, and manuals which circulated among craftsmen of the print shop.

The printer-editor labored in the West, remote from the eastern centers of journalism — from the type foundry and the paper mill, from the journals which furnished so much of the news, and under the handicap of an irregular and uncertain freight and mail delivery. Yet these hardships of the frontier did not deter him from issuing a prospectus and printing a newspaper before even a sufficiently compact and literate population had settled in the region to subscribe to the newspaper.

There is a paradox in the character of the pioneer editor: he was individualistic and eccentric, and yet he rarely varied much from the norms of the community. Perhaps this paradox can only exist when the community is made up of individualists. To all however, the editor asserted his independence. He felt little loyalty toward his fellow editors. He treated them as rivals, heaped reproach on them, and tried to take away their business. Sometimes he developed this same independent attitude toward his readers. The editor believed that newspapers were great contributions to civilization, and since his paper was undersubscribed and many of the subscriptions he had were unpaid for, he often berated the reading public when he felt he was not appreciated. In any case, the editor denied the right of any other, whether rival editor or reader, to prescribe a course for him.

In spite of his independence, the editor was a rather passive leader in society. He did not carry on very many sustained crusades, except in politics, nor conceive many new reforms for the improvement of society. News and format remained monotonous year in and year out. Society forced changes upon him; he did not change society. He stood among the colorful men striving for recognition and influence in frontier society; but changing conditions of journalism, his own individualitic personality, his itineracy, and his lax business methods deprived him of the stature he sought. While he advertised himself as a promoter of his region, his loyalty shifted from community to community as he moved about.

At the same time the pioneer editor, believing his newspaper essential to democratic government, felt a deep personal commitment to popular government and to freedom of the press. He played a primary role in establishing and transplanting laws and customs to the West, and in the building of new governments. Tocqueville termed the American press as "the chief democratic instrument of freedom." [1]

What was the impact of the frontier environment upon journalism? Before answering that question, several factors of eastern origin must be noted. The pioneer journalist did not forget the example and traditions of such fellow journalists as Benjamin Franklin, William Cobbett, Philip Freneau, Joseph Dennie, and Benjamin Franklin Bache. Also, he came into the frontier environment already trained as a craftsman of the "art preservative," now several centuries old. He could not forget the traditions of his craft, though the frontier produced considerable strain upon these traditions, perhaps weakened them enough to allow the business-industrial-technological revolution to take over. And, finally, much of the news was of eastern origin.

And yet the pioneer editor lived and worked in a world that was competitive, physically hard, combative, and uninstitutionalized, a world that provided only subsistence, and required hard manual labor — a primitive world. He strove for vigor and strength of expression in the conduct of his journal. When Edward Charless and Nathaniel Paschall retired from the *Missouri Republican*, their fellow editor, Abel Rathbone Corbin of the *Missouri Argus*, complimented them on the energy, firmness, and perseverance with which they had supported their position in public affairs.[2] This was the environment of frontier journalism.

The end of frontier journalism came slowly and unevenly. The transformation to the modern era began as early as 1836 with the establishment of the first daily in St. Louis. Other developments soon followed — the adoption of the power press, larger capital investments, more complex business organization, the rise of professional standards, the forging of a code of personal and business ethics, the revolution in local news, the decline in political emphasis, the transportation and communications revolution. Newspapering ceased to be a way of life. Profit became an end in itself. Business values replaced craft values. The Civil War in Missouri produced a great crisis: suspensions, confiscations, destruction, and censorship punctuated the history of Missouri journalism in that period. At the conclusion of the conflict, as the editors recovered their presses and rearranged their pied type, they discovered themselves in a new political and economic world, and soon they began to discover a new journalistic world as well.

NOTES

PROLOGUE

1. *Missouri Gazette* (St. Louis), March 21, April 4, 11, 1811.

2. L. C. Gray, *History of Agriculture in the Southern United States to 1860* (Washington, 1933), I, 380.

3. *Missouri Gazette* (St. Louis), March 21, 1811.

4. U. S. Bureau of the Census, *U. S. Census of Population: 1960*, Vol. I: *Characteristics of the Population*, Part A, "Number of Inhabitants" (Washington, 1961), pp. 27–29, Table 1.

5. W. B. Napton, *Past and Present of Saline County, Missouri* (Indianapolis, 1901), p. 324; *History of Saline County, Missouri* (St. Louis, 1881), pp. 148, 152.

6. John L. Peyton in Warren S. Tryon, comp. and ed., *A Mirror for Americans* (Chicago, 1952), III, 599. The newspaper editor was Mr. Windett, but I am unable to otherwise identify him.

7. U. S. Bureau of the Census, *U. S. Census of Population: 1960*, pp. 27–29, Table 1.

8. See Gray, *History of Agriculture in the Southern United States*, I, 443–44.

9. James N. Primm, *Economic Policy in a Frontier State: Missouri* (Cambridge, 1954), pp. 77–113.

10. *Ibid.*, pp. 18, 24–26, 48–71.

11. These changes are summarized in the last chapter of the book.

12. J. M. Peck, *A New Guide for Emigrants to the West* (2d ed.; Boston, 1837), pp. 119–21.

13. *Missouri Gazette* (St. Louis), March 21, 1811.
14. William Darby, *The Emigrant's Guide to the Western and Southwestern States and Territories* (New York, 1818), p. 303.

CHAPTER 1

1. I. Thomas, *The History of Printing in America* (2d ed; Albany, 1874), II, 305. Thomas' first edition appeared in 1810. *Ibid.*, I, ix.
2. *Missouri Gazette* (St. Louis), September 13, 1820.
3. Governor [James] Wilkinson to Secretary of State [Madison], September 7, 1805, C. E. Carter, comp. and ed., *The Territorial Papers of the United States, The Territory of Louisiana-Missouri, 1803–1806* (Washington, 1948), XIII, 196; D. C. McMurtrie, *Joseph Charless, Pioneer Printer of St. Louis* (Chicago, 1931), pp. 12–15.
4. C. S. Brigham, *History and Bibliography of American News-Papers, 1690–1820* (Worcester, 1947), I, 144; D. C. McMurtrie, "The Early Career of Joseph Charless," *Missouri Historical Review* (July, 1932), XXVI, 352–53.
5. Clark Collection (Missouri Historical Society, St. Louis), Governor Meriwether Lewis to William Clark, May 29, 1808.
6. Bernard G. Farrar Day Book (Missouri Historical Society, St. Louis), June 27, July 2, 1808; for a fuller treatment of Charless see W. H. Lyon, "Joseph Charless, The Father of Missouri Journalism," *Bulletin of the Missouri Historical Society* (January, 1961), XVII, 133–45.
7. Meriwether Lewis Anderson Collection (Missouri Historical Society, St. Louis), Meriwether Lewis Receipt Book, July 22, December 28, 1808, March 7, May 5, 1809.
8. *Missouri Gazette* (St. Louis), January 4, 1809.
9. *Ibid.*, July 26, 1808, January 4, 1809.
10. *Ibid.*, January 21, 1813, August 2, September 13, 1820.
11. *Ibid.*, November 12, 1814, January 21, 1815.
12. *Ibid.*, September 28, 1816; Brigham, *History and Bibliography*, I, 432–34.
13. *Missouri Gazette* (St. Louis), September 6, 1817, July 24, 1818, September 8, 1819.
14. *Ibid.*, August 5, 1815.
15. *Missouri Argus* (St. Louis), October 9, 1835.
16. United States Census Office, *Compendium of the Enumeration of the Inhabitants and Statistics of the United States . . .* [Sixth Census, 1840] (Washington, 1841), p. 319. The census does not appear to be entirely accurate. Also, it must be remembered that a newspaper establishment had several editions usually — a daily and weekly, or a weekly and a tri-weekly, etc.

17. United States Census Office, *The Seventh Census of the United States: 1850* (Washington, 1853), pp. lxv, 682.

18. *The St. Louis Republic*, July 12, 1908.

19. *St. Louis Enquirer*, May 5, 1817.

20. Various letters and petitions on this subject are found in Carter, *Territorial Papers*, XV, 529, 530–31, 532, 539, 543, 553, 573, 574, 641–42, 683; Brigham, *History and Bibliography*, I, 431–32.

21. *Independent Patriot* (Jackson), December 23, 1820, May 19, 1821, August 31, 1822, March 4, 1826; Brigham, *History and Bibliography*, I, 433.

22. *Missouri Intelligencer* (Franklin), April 24, 1824.

23. On Calvin Gunn see *ibid.*, October 28, 1825, and *ibid.*, Fayette, November 18, 1828; *Jeffersonian Republican* (Jefferson City), September 19, 1840.

24. C. S. B. [C. S. Brigham], "Daniel Hewitt's List of Newspapers and Periodicals in the United States in 1828," *Proceedings of the American Antiquarian Society* (October, 1934), n.s., XLIV, 381–82.

25. *Missouri Gazette* (St. Louis), November 17, 1819, February 9, 1820; *Missouri Republican* (St. Louis), October 22, 1823, April 2, 1823 (a notice to printers of sale, which must be from M'Cloud), June 15, 1826, February 1, 1827 (mentioned in a law of Missouri).

26. McMurtrie, *Joseph Charless*, 35; *Missouri Republican* (St. Louis), November 1, 1827, March 18, 1828.

27. *Missouri Intelligencer* (Franklin), April 30, 1821; *Missouri Republican* (St. Louis), March 20, 1822.

28. *Missouri Intelligencer* (Franklin), January 18, August 12, 1825; *Missouri Republican* (St. Louis), October 26, 1826, January 11, 1827, November 7, 21, December 5, 1825, November 16, 1826.

29. *Missouri Republican* (St. Louis), December 9, 23, 1828.

30. *Missouri Intelligencer* (Fayette), November 23, 1827.

31. *Ibid.*, February 27, 1829.

32. *Missouri Republican* (St. Louis), June 21, July 12, 1827, April 29, 1828.

33. *Missouri Intelligencer* (Fayette), February 27, October 2, 1829, and *ibid.* (Columbia), August 9, 1834; *ibid.* (Fayette), February 27, 1829, March 19, 1830, and *ibid.* (Columbia), December 22, 1832.

34. *Ibid.* (Columbia), September 27, December 27, 1834.

35. *Ibid.*, May 2, November 21, 1831; *Missouri Argus* (St. Louis), May 29, 1835.

36. *Jeffersonian Republican* (Jefferson City), January 25, 1834; *Missouri Argus* (St. Louis) November 27, 1835.

37. See p. 31.

38. *Missouri Intelligencer* (Columbia), May 18, 1833.

39. *Jeffersonian Republican* (Jefferson City), March 19, 1836, March 19, 22, 1839; *Liberty Weekly Tribune*, April 25, 1856.

40. *Missouri Argus* (St. Louis), June 14, 1839.

41. *Jeffersonian Republican* (Jefferson City), January 11, 1834; *Missouri Intelligencer* (Columbia), January 31, April 4, May 23, 1835.

42. *Missouri Intelligencer* (Columbia), May 23, 1835; *Missouri Argus* (St. Louis), May 26, September 27, 1837, November 22, 1839, June 1, 2, 9, 13, 17, August 17, November 9, 1840; W. N. Chambers, *Old Bullion Benton* (Boston, 1956), pp. 260–61.

43. *Missouri Argus* (St. Louis), May 30, 1840.

44. U. S. Census Office [Sixth Census, 1840], p. 319.

45. *Ibid.*

46. E. E. Sparlin, "The Jefferson Inquirer" (unpublished Master's thesis, University of Missouri, 1932), p. 13.

47. U. S. Census Office, *The Seventh Census*, pp. lxv, 682.

48. *The Daily Tribune* (Jefferson City), October 30,1891; D. G. Brown, "Early St. Louis Newspapers" (unpublished Master's thesis, Washington University, 1931), pp. 89–90.

49. *Liberty Weekly Tribune*, June 26, 1857.

50. *Missouri Intelligencer* (Columbia), April 13, July 27, September 14, 1833, January 11, September 13, 20, December 27, 1834; *The Western Emigrant* (Boonville), February 14, 1839.

51. *History of Saline County, Missouri* (St. Louis, 1881), pp. 389–91.

52. Leonard MSS (State Historical Society of Missouri, Columbia), Charless and Paschall to T. J. Boggs, April 26, 1831, and T. J. Boggs to A. Leonard, April 30, 1831.

53. *Missouri Gazette* (St. Louis), September 20, 1817.

54. Dunklin Papers (University of Missouri, Columbia), J. W. Miller to D. Dunklin, March 8, 1832.

55. *Ibid.*, D. Dunklin to Governor Miller, March 31, 1832.

56. *Ibid.*, J. Steele to D. Dunklin, February 25, March 16, 1832.

57. *Ibid.*, J. Steele to D. Dunklin, April 9, 16, 26, 1832, and D. Dunklin to J. Steele, April 14, 1832.

58. *Ibid.*, D. Dunklin to Governor Miller, April 14, 1832, D. Dunklin to J. Steele, March 8, 31, 1832, A. L. Magenis to D. Dunklin, April 30, 1832; Brown, "Early St. Louis Newspapers," p. 85; Missouri, *Journal of the House*, 7th General Assembly, 1st Session (St. Louis: John Steele, Free Press Office, 1833).

59. Dunklin Papers, D. Dunklin to F. H. Martin, August 21, 1834, and J. Jameson to D. Dunklin, September 11, 1834.

60. Sappington Papers (State Historical Society of Missouri, Columbia), R. W. Wells to M. M. Marmaduke, August 23, 1834; *Jeffersonian Republican* (Jefferson City), December 27, 1834.

61. Dunklin Papers, D. Dunklin to F. H. Martin, August 21, September 17, 1834, A. G. Harrison, P. G. Glover, and J. B. Thompson to D. Dunklin, September 11, 1834, J. Jameson to D. Dunklin,

September 11, 1834, A. W. Manning to D. Dunklin, September 13, 1834, D. Dunklin to A. W. Manning, September 26, 1834, A. L. Magenis to D. Dunklin, September 13, 1834, A. G. Harrison to D. Dunklin, August 31, 1835; *Missouri Intelligencer* (Columbia), December 27, 1834, April 4, 1835.

62. Dunklin Papers, A. L. Magenis to [D. Dunklin], and enclosure, September 13, 1834, and D. Dunklin to F. H. Martin, September 26, 1835.

63. Leonard MSS, J. H. Birch to A. Leonard, December 17, 1839.

64. L. O. Banks, "Latter Day Saint Journalism" (unpublished Master's thesis, University of Missouri, 1948), pp. 11–37.

65. *Ibid.*, pp. 125–36. The name of this paper was *The Elder's Journal*.

66. *Missouri Argus* (St. Louis), July 22, 29, 1836; H. Martineau, *Society in America* (4th ed.; New York, 1837), I, 112.

CHAPTER 2

1. An original of this prospectus may be found in the Pierre Chouteau Collection (Missouri Historical Society, St. Louis).

2. *Jeffersonian Republican* (Jefferson City), July 14, 1838.

3. W. N. Chambers, "Thomas Hart Benton: Editor," *Missouri Historical Review* (July, 1952), XLVI, 336; see also *St. Louis Enquirer*, April 21, 1819.

4. Prospectus of Duff Green and P. H. Ford for *St. Louis Enquirer* in *Independent Patriot* (Jackson), February 28, 1824; see also James C. Cummins in *Missouri Gazette* (St. Louis), December 6, 1820.

5. *Missouri Intelligencer* (Franklin), April 23, 1819.

6. Dunklin Papers (University of Missouri, Columbia), D. Dunklin to C. Kemlee [*sic*], June 28, 1831.

7. *Missouri Intelligencer* (Franklin), August 5, 1822.

8. *Missouri Republican* (St. Louis), October 22, 1823.

9. *Missouri Intelligencer* (Columbia), November 20, 1830.

10. *Missouri Gazette* (St. Louis), September 13, 1820.

11. Prospectus of Robert M'Cloud for the Ste. Genevieve *Missouri Sentinel*, in *Independent Patriot* (Jackson), November 6, 1826.

12. *Jefferson Inquirer* (Jefferson City), September 10, 1840.

13. Prospectus of William Ridenbaugh for *St. Joseph Gazette*, April 25, 1845, in F. M. Pumphrey, "The Old St. Jo Gazette," *Missouri Historical Review* (October, 1943), XXXVIII, 33.

14. *Independent Patriot* (Jackson), November 6, 1826.

15. *Ibid.*, February 28, 1824.

16. Chambers, "Thomas Hart Benton: Editor," pp. 337–38.

17. *St. Louis Enquirer*, April 21, May 5, 1819; prospectus of Nathaniel Patten in C. E. Carter, comp. and ed., *The Territorial Papers of the United States, The Territory of Louisiana-Missouri, 1815–1821* (Washington, 1951), XV, 530.

18. *The Metropolitan* (Jefferson City), May 4, 1847.

19. H. V. Funk, "A History of the *California* (Missouri) *Democrat* 1858–1958" (unpublished Master's thesis, University of Missouri, 1957), p. 19.

20. *Missouri Gazette* (St. Louis), September 13, 1820.

21. *Independent Patriot* (Jackson), November 6, 1826.

22. *Missouri Intelligencer* (Franklin), August 5, 1825.

23. *Independent Patriot* (Jackson), March 4, 1826.

24. *Ibid.*, December 23, 1820.

25. *St. Louis Enquirer*, April 21, 1819.

26. *Boonville Observer*, March 17, 1846.

27. *The Weekly Tribune* (Liberty), April 4, 1846.

28. *Missouri Intelligencer* (Columbia), June 23, 1832.

29. *Ibid.* (Fayette), May 22, 1829.

30. The preceding analysis was based upon various prospectuses, in addition to those cited in footnotes.

31. *St. Louis Enquirer*, April 21, 1819.

32. *Boonville Observer*, April 25, 1850.

33. *Missouri Intelligencer* (Franklin), August 5, 1822.

34. B. E. Birkhead, "A Study of the *Missouri Gazette* through the Editorship of Its Founder, Joseph Charless" (unpublished Master's thesis, University of Missouri, 1945), pp. 80–81.

35. See *Boonville Observer*, April 25, 1850, and following; *Missouri Gazette* (St. Louis), October 24, 1810, May 16, 1811; E. Johnson, "The Economic Development of the Boonslick Country as Reflected in the *Missouri Intelligencer*" (unpublished Master's thesis, University of Missouri, 1931), p. 21.

36. G. F. Lemmer, *Norman J. Colman and Colman's Rural World* (Columbia, Missouri, 1953), pp. 18–28, 52.

37. J. H. French, "Community Service Activities of the *Missouri Statesman* from 1843 to 1863" (unpublished Master's thesis, University of Missouri, 1938), p. 119.

38. *Missouri Intelligencer* (Franklin), July 1, 1820. See also J. W. Ridings, "Editorial Policies of the *Missouri Intelligencer*" (unpublished Master's thesis, University of Missouri, 1928), pp. 70, 96.

39. *Missouri Republican* (St. Louis), March 1, 1824; see also *The Western Emigrant* (Boonville), January 17, 1839, *Jeffersonian Republican* (Jefferson City), August 24, 1839, *The Weekly Tribune* (Liberty), December 26, 1846.

40. *Missouri Gazette* (St. Louis), November 13, 1818.

41. *Missouri Republican* (St. Louis), February 2, 10, October 4, 1824.

42. Ridings, *"Missouri Intelligencer,"* Plate I after p. 103.

43. See French, *"Missouri Statesman," passim.* For an account of Switzler's role in organizing the first state press association see pp. 127–131.

44. Johnson, "Economic Development of the Boonslick Country, pp. 17–20, 60–65.

45. *Missouri Intelligencer* (Franklin), June 18, 1825.

46. D. G. Brown, "Early St. Louis Newspapers, 1808–1850" (unpublished Master's thesis, Washington University, 1931), pp. 21, 49, 53, 57–58, 76, 81.

47. Johnson, "Economic Development of the Boonslick Country," pp. 65–67.

48. A. de Tocqueville, *Democracy in America* (New York, 1945), I, 211. First published in 1835.

49. J. Viles, "Old Franklin: A Frontier Town of the Twenties," *Mississippi Valley Historical Review* (March, 1923), IX, 269–82.

50. Patten in *St. Charles Clarion* reprinted in *Missouri Argus* (St. Louis), May 26, 1837.

CHAPTER 3

1. Various documents on this subject are in C. E. Carter, comp. and ed., *The Territorial Papers of the United States, The Territory of Louisiana-Missouri, 1815–1821* (Washington, 1951), XV, 529, 539, 543, 553, 573–74, 641–42, 683; *Missouri Intelligencer* (Franklin), March 5, 1821.

2. *Missouri Republican* (St. Louis), December 13, 1824.

3. *Missouri Argus* (St. Louis), August 29, November 20, 1840.

4. *Missouri Intelligencer* (Fayette), October 2, 1829.

5. *Ibid.,* January 8, 1830.

6. *Ibid.* (Columbia), October 31, 1835.

7. See Charless statement in *Missouri Gazette* (St. Louis), July 31, 1813; but also *St. Louis Enquirer*, December 23, 30, 1818.

8. Charless to Acting Governor Pope, April 20, 1809, in Carter, *Territorial Papers*, XVI, 24–25; *Missouri Gazette* (St. Louis), February 15, 1810, and *passim*, April 18, 1811, and *passim*.

9. *Missouri Gazette* (St. Louis), January 21, 1815.

10. *Ibid.,* July 24, 1818; *St. Louis Enquirer*, December 23, 30, 1818.

11. Various documents may be found in Carter, *Territorial Papers*, XV, 112, 332–33, 573, 574, 683.

12. See *Missouri Gazette* (St. Louis), August 2, 1820, for Charless' side, and *Missouri Intelligencer* (Franklin), August 19, 1820, for Green's side.

13. *Missouri Republican* (St. Louis), December 13, 1824, Janu-

ary 10, 1825; Missouri, *Journal of the Senate*, 3rd General Assembly (St. Charles: Duff Green, 1825), pp. 55, 115, 149–50. In the footnotes to this chapter, in which the newspaper editor as the publisher of the public laws is discussed, full citation, including publisher as well as place and date, has been given.

14. *Missouri Intelligencer* (Columbia), September 27, 1834.

15. *Ibid.*, September 6, 1834; Dunklin Papers (University of Missouri, Columbia), Jameson to Dunklin, September 11, 1834.

16. *Missouri Intelligencer* (Columbia), May 23, 1835.

17. *Jefferson Inquirer* (Jefferson City), December 4, 18, 25, 1847, March 10, June 23, 30, 1849, May 11, June 1, 1850.

18. Leonard MSS (State Historical Society of Missouri, Columbia), Rollins to Leonard, February 5, 1851, and Broadhead to Leonard, February 7, 1851.

19. *Jefferson Inquirer* (Jefferson City), July 30, 1853; 18 *Missouri Reports* 333; for a general account of the Lusks see E. E. Sparlin, "The *Jefferson Inquirer*" (unpublished Master's thesis, University of Missouri, 1932).

20. Missouri, *Laws of a Public and General Nature . . . up to the Year 1824* (Jefferson City: W. Lusk and Son, 1842, p. 998.

21. Missouri, *Laws of the State of Missouri; Revised and Digested by Authority of the General Assembly* (St. Louis: E. Charless, 1825), II, 648–53.

22. Missouri, *Journal of the House*, 10th General Assembly, 1st Session ([Jefferson City: Calvin Gunn, 1839]), p. 234.

23. *Missouri Intelligencer* (Columbia), December 3, 1831.

24. Missouri, *Laws of the State of Missouri*, 7th General Assembly, 1st Session (Jefferson City: [Calvin Gunn, 1833]), pp. 89–90.

25. *Ibid.*, p. 152.

26. *Missouri Argus* (St. Louis), May 25, December 18, 1835, October 28, 1836; *Missouri Intelligencer* (Columbia), March 14, 1835; Missouri, *Journal of the House*, 9th General Assembly, 1st Session (Bowling Green: at the Office of the *Salt River Journal*, 1837), pp. 107, 112–14.

27. *Jeffersonian Republican* (Jefferson City), August 24, 1839.

28. Missouri, *Journal of the Senate*, 13th General Assembly, 1st Session (Jefferson City: Gunn, Hammond, and Main, 1845), Appendix, pp. 52–56.

29. Missouri, *The Revised Statutes of the State of Missouri, Revised and Digested by the Thirteenth General Assembly* (St. Louis: J. W. Dougherty, 1845), pp. 907–12.

30. Missouri, *Journal of the Senate*, 14th General Assembly, 1st Session (Jefferson City: James Lusk, 1847), pp. 34, 458, Appendix, p. 249; *ibid.*, 15th General Assembly, 1st Session (Jefferson City: Hampton L. Boon, 1848), pp. 23, 52.

CHAPTER 4

1. "Fourth Estate," *The Oxford English Dictionary* (Oxford, 1933). Carlyle had used the term earlier in 1837 in his *The French Revolution.*

2. B. Fay, *Notes on the American Press at the End of the Eighteenth Century* (New York, 1927), pp. 9–14.

3. *Missouri Gazette* (St. Louis), December 6, 1820.

4. Leonard MSS (State Historical Society of Missouri, Columbia), A. S. Mitchell to A. Leonard, April 18, 1851, February 10, 1852.

5. *Ibid.,* W. F. Birch to A. Leonard, December 22, 1831, January 20, 1832.

6. *Jefferson Inquirer* (Jefferson City), December 24, 1840; *The Weekly Tribune* (Liberty), April 4, 1846; see the prospectus of Middleton and Need for the *Boonville Herald* in *Missouri Intelligencer* (Columbia), April 13, 1833, and Nathaniel Patten's later comment, *ibid.,* September 14, 1833.

7. H. V. Funk, "A History of the *California* (Missouri) *Democrat,* 1858–1958" (unpublished Master's thesis, University of Missouri, 1957), p. 17.

8. W. N. Chambers, *Old Bullion Benton* (Boston, 1956), p. 149.

9. Leonard MSS, J. H. Birch to A. Leonard, December 17, 1839.

10. Dunklin Papers (University of Missouri, Columbia), J. Miller to D. Dunklin, March 8, 1832.

11. Leonard MSS, J. O. Broadhead to A. Leonard, March 16, 1851.

12. Dunklin Papers, D. Dunklin to F. H. Martin, August 21, 1834.

13. *Missouri Republican* (St. Louis), May 10, 1827.

14. *Ibid.,* May 17, 1827.

15. *Missouri Intelligencer* (Fayette), May 17, 1827.

16. *Ibid.,* March 14, April 4, 1828.

17. *Ibid.* (Columbia), December 22, 1832.

18. C. M. Thompson, "Elections and Election Machinery In Illinois, 1818–1848," *Journal of the Illinois State Historical Society* (January, 1915), VII, 379–80.

19. Dunklin Papers, A. G. Harrison, P. G. Glover, and J. B. Thompson to D. Dunklin, September 11, 1834, and J. Jameson to D. Dunklin, September 11, 1834, F. H. Martin to D. Dunklin, November 14, 1835, D. Dunklin to Editor of the St. Louis *Argus* [Corbin], September 26, 1835.

20. *Ibid.,* A. R. Corbin to D. Dunklin, September 18, November 23, 1835.

21. *Ibid.,* D. Dunklin to C. Kemlee [*sic*], June 28, 1831.

22. *Ibid.,* D. Dunklin to Editor of the St. Louis *Argus* [Corbin], September 26, 1835.

23. *Ibid.*, J. W. Miller to D. Dunklin, August 22, 1831.

24. Sibley Papers (Missouri Historical Society, St. Louis), A. B. Chambers to G. C. Sibley, May 12, 1840.

25. Chambers, *Old Bullion Benton*, pp. 260–61, 268–69, 283, 316–17; *Jefferson Inquirer* (Jefferson City), October 5, 1843.

26. *Missouri Intelligencer* (Fayette), October 2, 1829, and *ibid.* (Columbia), May 16, 1835; *Jefferson Inquirer* (Jefferson City), June 1, 1850; *Liberty Weekly Tribune*, November 28, 1851; *The Daily Tribune* (Jefferson City), January 13, 1878.

27. *Missouri Intelligencer* (Fayette), October 2, 1829.

28. Dunklin Papers, D. Dunklin to C. Kemlee [*sic*], June 28, 1831, and J. W. Miller to D. Dunklin, August 22, 1831.

29. Ibid., D. Dunklin to F. H. Martin, August 21, 1834, D. Dunklin to [?], December 18, 1835.

30. *Missouri Argus* (St. Louis), July 22, 1836.

31. *Missouri Republican* (St. Louis), November 18, 1828; *Missouri Intelligencer* (Fayette), November 28, 1828.

32. *Missouri Republican* (St. Louis), December 9, 23, 1828.

33. *Missouri Argus* (St. Louis), March 11, 1836.

34. *Missouri Argus* (St. Louis), March 30, 1840; *Jefferson Inquirer* (Jefferson City), May 2, October 24, 1844; D. G. Brown, "Early St. Louis Newspapers, 1808–1850" (unpublished Master's thesis, Washington University, 1931), pp. 26, 55, 65.

CHAPTER 5

1. C. S. Brigham, *Journals and Journeymen* (Philadelphia, 1950), p. 69.

2. *Missouri Intelligencer* (Franklin), April 23, 1819.

3. Missouri, *The Revised Statutes of the State of Missouri, Revised and Digested by the Thirteenth General Assembly* (St. Louis: J. W. Dougherty, 1845), pp. 1011, 342.

4. *Missouri Gazette* (St. Louis), October 31, 1810.

5. *Ibid.*, February 28, 1811.

6. *Ibid.*, May 17, 1820.

7. *Missouri Intelligencer* (Fayette), January 18, 1828.

8. *Missouri Argus* (St. Louis), November 22, 1839, June 1, 2, August 17, November 9, 1840.

9. *Missouri Gazette* (St. Louis), July 16, 1814.

10. A. J. Stansbury, *Report of the Trial of James H. Peck* (Boston, 1833), pp. 40, 353; *Missouri Gazette* (St. Louis), May 17, 1820.

11. Missouri, *Journal of the House*, 1st General Assembly, 1st Session (St. Louis: Edward Charless [at the *Republican* office], 1822), pp. 66, 89–90.

12. Stansbury, *Report of the Trial of James H. Peck*, pp. 353–54.

Since no date or names are given, the printers of the *St. Louis Enquirer* could have been P. H. Ford and William Orr, or Ford and Jacob Stine, or Ford and Duff Green.

13. Stansbury, *Report of the Trial of James H. Peck*, pp. 1–4, 15, 50–51. "A Citizen" is printed on the last named pages, and Judge Peck's decision in the Soulard case is given in the *Missouri Republican* (St. Louis), March 30, 1826.

14. Stansbury, *Report of the Trial of James H. Peck*, pp. 21–35, 73, 85–101, 481 and following.

15. *Ibid.*, pp. 39–40, 102–3.

16. *Ibid.*, pp. 474, 591.

17. D. G. Brown, "Early St. Louis Newspapers, 1808–1850" (unpublished Master's thesis, Washington University, 1931), p. 22.

18. *Jeffersonian Republican* (Jefferson City), March 19, 1836; *Missouri Argus* (St. Louis), April 1, May 13, November 11, 1836, February 17, 1837.

19. Leonard MSS (State Historical Society of Missouri, Columbia), B. H. Reeves to A. Leonard, January 1, 1835.

20. *Jefferson Inquirer* (Jefferson City), January 12, 1843.

21. *The Weekly Tribune* (Liberty), August 3, November 23, 1849; *Liberty Weekly Tribune*, May 23, 1851, March 24, 1854.

22. *Missouri Republican* (St. Louis), October 24, 1825.

23. *Ibid.*, October 31, November 7, 11, 1825; *Missouri Intelligencer* (Franklin), November 4, 18, 1825.

24. *Missouri Republican* (St. Louis), October 26, 1826.

25. *Missouri Intelligencer* (Fayette), January 8, 1830.

26. *Jeffersonian Republican* (Jefferson City), January 11, 1834; Dunklin Papers (University of Missouri, Columbia), S. W. Foreman to D. Dunklin, August 26, 1833; *Missouri Intelligencer* (Columbia), February 22, June 21, 28, 1834, January 10, 1835.

27. *Keemle and Field v. Richard F. Sass*, 12 *Missouri Reports*, 499. In the New York case, James Fenimore Cooper sued Horace Greeley (as well as two other editors, Thurlow Weed and James Watson Webb) for statements critical of his novels. He received a judgment of $200 from Greeley.

28. *Missouri Gazette* (St. Louis), August 9, September 6, 1817; Acting Secretary of War [George Graham] to T. A. Smith, October 27, 1817, C. E. Carter, comp. and ed., *The Territorial Papers of the United States, The Territory of Louisiana-Missouri, 1815–1821* (Washington, 1951), XV, 320; Delegate [John] Scott to President [James] Monroe, February 4, 1818, with enclosed "A Statement [to the President] of Several Citizens Relative to the Recent Election held in the Territory," *ibid.*, pp. 341–42; Judge [J. B. C.] Lucas to Secretary of State [J. Q.] Adams, May 1, 1818, *ibid.*, pp. 386–87.

29. *Missouri Gazette* (St. Louis), February 6, 1818.

30. Dunklin Papers, Order No. 5, Headquarters of the Army, Adjutant General's Office, Washington, January 28, 1833.

31. *Missouri Intelligencer* (Fayette), November 2, 9, 1827, January 18, 1828.

32. *Missouri Gazette* (St. Louis), July 22, 1815.

33. *Ibid.*, August 28, 1818.

34. See p. 76.

35. *Missouri Intelligencer* (Fayette), June 27, 1828.

36. *Missouri Argus* (St. Louis), February 16, 1838.

37. See p. 75.

38. *Jefferson Inquirer* (Jefferson City), June 25, 1853.

39. E. D. Hall, "William Franklin Switzler" (unpublished Master's thesis, University of Missouri, 1951), pp. 73–74.

40. *Jeffersonian Republican* (Jefferson City), September 16, 1843.

41. *Missouri Argus* (St. Louis), March 11, 1836.

CHAPTER 6

1. Matthew Lyon to John Edgar, March 11, 1809, C. E. Carter, comp. and ed., *The Territorial Papers of the United States, The Territory of Illinois 1809–1814* (Washington, 1948), XVI, 18.

2. *Missouri Gazette* (St. Louis), March 21, 1812.

3. *Ibid.*, April 19,1810.

4. P. Chouteau Maffitt Collection (Missouri Historical Society, St. Louis), J. Charless to P. Chouteau, July 10, 1810.

5. *Missouri Gazette* (St. Louis), August 15, 1812.

6. *Missouri Intelligencer* (Franklin), August 5, 1823; *ibid.* (Fayette), March 19, 26, April 16, 30, 1831, February 14, 1835; *Missouri Gazette* (St. Louis), July 26, 1810, August 12, 1815; *Independent Patriot* (Jackson), November 22, 1823, May 28, 1825.

7. *Boonville Observer*, March 17, 1846; *The Western Emigrant* (Boonville), October 3, 1839; *Jefferson Inquirer* (Jefferson City), September 10, 1840; *The Weekly Tribune* (Liberty), March 23, 1849.

8. Dunklin Papers (University of Missouri, Columbia), C. Keemle to D. Dunklin, September 23, 1831.

9. E. E. Sparlin, "The *Jefferson Inquirer*" (unpublished Master's thesis, University of Missouri, 1932), p. 27.

10. *Liberty Weekly Tribune*, February 18, 1859.

11. John and William L. Long Papers (Missouri Historical Society, St. Louis), receipt of Joseph Charless to John Long, undated, but with the date of October 15, 1814, mentioned; *Missouri Gazette* (St. Louis), April 19, December 19, 1810, September 12, 1812, January 2, 1813; *Missouri Register* (Boonville) December 12, 1843.

12. *The Weekly Tribune* (Liberty), December 17, 1847.

13. *Boonville Observer*, March 17, 1846; *Missouri Argus* (St Louis), March 5, 1840.

14. *Missouri Gazette* (St. Louis), November 13, 1818.

15. *Missouri Argus* (St. Louis), October 25, 1838.

16. Prospectus of Charless, typewritten facsimile, located in first volume of *Missouri Gazette* in State Historical Society of Missouri, Columbia.

17. *Independent Patriot* (Jackson), December 23, 1820.

18. *Jefferson Inquirer* (Jefferson City), September 10, 1840; *The Weekly Tribune* (Liberty), March 23, 1849.

19. Mark Twain, *Mark Twain's Autobiography* (New York, 1924), II, 285.

20. Reprinted from *Louisiana Herald* in *Liberty Weekly Tribune*, May 13, 1859; *Boonville Observer*, February 17, March 31, 1846.

21. *The Western Emigrant* (Boonville), October 3, 1839.

22. *Jefferson Inquirer* (Jefferson City), September 10, 1840; see also *Missouri Argus* (St. Louis), March 11, 1836.

23. *Missouri Intelligencer* (Franklin), March 5, 1821, April 16, 1822; Leonard MSS (State Historical Society of Missouri, Columbia), T. J. Miller and Company to A. Leonard, September 11, 1832; *Missouri Gazette* (St. Louis), January 3, 1821.

24. *Missouri Republican* (St. Louis), April 26, 1824, July 1, 1828.

25. Leonard MSS, T. J. Miller and Company to A. Leonard, September 11, 1832; *Missouri Republican* (St. Louis), July 1, 1828; *Missouri Intelligencer* (Columbia), August 30, 1834; *Missouri Argus* (St. Louis), October 28, 1836.

26. *The St. Louis Republic*, July 12, 1908; Memoranda [*sic*] dated March, 1840, of J. T. Cleveland in flyleaf of bound volume of *Missouri Intelligencer*, 1822–24, Missouri Historical Society. Cleveland could possibly have been mistaken, and for that side of the question see C. V. R. [Charles van Ravenswaay], "The Cover: Pioneer Presses in Missouri," *Bulletin of the Missouri Historical Society* (April, 1951), VII, 296–301, and Missouri Intelligencer Press, Alphabetical Files, Missouri Historical Society. From the description and the commentary of the expert in the Smithsonian Institution, it might appear that the press was rebuilt for Patten's use, and thus it is not necessary to discard Cleveland's statement as inaccurate.

27. C. S. Brigham, *Journals and Journeymen* (Philadelphia, 1950), pp. 19–22.

28. *Missouri Gazette* (St. Louis), October 20, 1819, September 13, 1820.

29. *Missouri Intelligencer* (Franklin), August 5, 1823.

30. *The Western Emigrant* (Boonville), February 14, 1839.

31. Leonard MSS, A. S. Mitchell to A. Leonard, March 29, 1852.

32. H. V. Funk, "A History of the *California* (Missouri) *Demo-*

crat" (unpublished Master's thesis, University of Missouri, 1957), p. 16; Dunklin Papers, A. L. Magenis to [D. Dunklin, with enclosure by C. Keemle], September 13, 1834.

33. Sparlin, *"Jefferson Inquirer,"* pp. 26–27.

34. *Missouri Intelligencer* (Fayette), November 21, 1828, and *ibid.,* (Columbia), May 25, 1833.

35. See the business regulations of the Missouri Editors' Convention quoted in *Liberty Weekly Tribune,* June 24, 1859.

36. *Liberty Weekly Tribune,* March 23, 1849; *Jefferson Inquirer* (Jefferson City), February 18, 1846; and Funk, *"California Democrat,"* p. 220.

37. *Liberty Weekly Tribune,* February 18, 1859.

38. *Missouri Gazette* (St. Louis), September 28, 1816.

39. Dunklin Papers, C. Keemle to D. Dunklin, September 23, 1831; David Rice Atchison Papers (University of Missouri, Columbia), J. W. Denver to D. R. Atchison, April 12, 1850.

40. *Missouri Argus* (St. Louis), November 22, 1839.

41. *Liberty Weekly Tribune,* April 25, 1856.

CHAPTER 7

1. C. S. Brigham, *History and Bibliography of American Newspapers, 1690–1820* (Worcester, 1947), I, 180; *Missouri Intelligencer* (Franklin), February 15, 22, 1825.

2. N. Patten to Secretary of State [Adams], March 24, 1819, C. E. Carter, comp. and ed., *The Territorial Papers of the United States, The Territory of Louisiana-Missouri, 1815–1821* (Washington, 1951), XV, 529–30.

3. *Ibid.,* June 24, 1819, pp. 543–44.

4. *Missouri Intelligencer* (Franklin), June 4, July 23, September 25, 1821, August 5, 1822, and *ibid.* (Columbia), December 22, 1832. Documents of interest from the Howard County Court House, are reprinted in A. L. B. Korn, "Major Benjamin Holliday," *Missouri Historical Review* (October, 1919), XIV, 21–25. Mrs. Korn insists that her ancestor, Major Benjamin Holliday, was the real founder and editor of the *Missouri Intelligencer.* According to her Patten came to Franklin, Missouri, in need of employment and begged Holliday to let him buy one-third interest. Documents now available in Carter, *Territorial Papers,* and in the Leonard MSS, cited next below, indicate she is in error.

5. Leonard MSS (State Historical Society of Missouri, Columbia), N. Patton [*sic*] and J. T. Cleveland Agreement, July 31, 1822, and J. T. Cleveland to A. Leonard, November 25, 1825. Documents which reveal Patten's indebtedness to his mother, sister, and others

are found in the Howard County Recorder's Office, Fayette, Books G, I, K, O, P, Q.

6. *Missouri Intelligencer* (Franklin), April 17, 24, May 15, 29, 1824.

7. *Ibid.* (Fayette), January 25, February 22, December 26, 1828, May 15, 1829, January 29, 1830, and *ibid.* (Columbia), February 5, 1831, August 30, 1834; U. S. Congress, Senate, 19th Cong., 2nd Sess., January 19, 1827, II, No. 25; U. S. Congress, House, 21st Cong., 1st Sess., January 6, 1830, I, No. 59; U. S. Congress, House, 22nd Cong., 1st Sess., February 8, 1832, III, No. 335; U. S. Congress, House, 23rd Cong., 1st Sess., December 20, 1833, I, No. 52; U. S. Congress, House, 24th Cong., 2nd Sess., February 22, 1837, II, No. 271; U. S. Congress, House, 29th Cong., 2nd Sess., February 28, 1846, II, No. 376; U. S. Congress, House, 32nd Cong., 1st Sess., July 30, 1852, I, No. 164.

8. *Missouri Intelligencer* (Columbia), February 21, December 5, 1835; Rollins Papers (State Historical Society of Missouri, Columbia), Thomas Miller to J. S. Rollins, April 16, 1836, Article of Agreement between Patten, Rollins, and Kirtley, October 10, 1835.

9. *Missouri Argus* (St. Louis), May 6, November 4, 1836; *Jeffersonian Republican* (Jefferson City), November 5, 1836.

10. *Missouri Gazette* (St. Louis), September 13, 1820. See discussion of Charless on pp. 13–16.

11. *Missouri Intelligencer* (Franklin), September 2, 1823; *Jeffersonian Republican* (Jefferson City), September 19, 1840.

12. Dunklin Papers (University of Missouri, Columbia), D. Dunklin to A. W. Manning, September 26, 1834.

13. *Missouri Gazette* (St. Louis), January 21, 1815.

14. *Missouri Argus* (St. Louis), June 19, 1835.

15. D. G. Brown, "Early St. Louis Newspapers, 1808–1850" (unpublished Master's thesis, Washington University, 1931), p. 45; Dunklin Papers, C. Keemle to D. Dunklin, September 23, 1831.

16. Mark Twain, *Mark Twain's Autobiography* (New York, 1924), II, 285.

17. *Missouri Herald* (Jackson), April 1, 1820; *Independent Patriot* (Jackson), May 19, 1821, August 31, 1822.

18. *Missouri Intelligencer* (Fayette), October 9, 1829.

19. Dunklin Papers, A. L. Magenis to [D. Dunklin with enclosure by C. Keemle], September 13, 1834.

20. H. V. Funk, "A History of the *California* (Missouri) *Democrat*" (unpublished Master's thesis, University of Missouri, 1958), p. 16.

21. *Liberty Weekly Tribune*, March 3, 1848.

22. E. E. Sparlin, "The *Jefferson Inquirer*" (unpublished Master's thesis, University of Missouri, 1932), p. 30.

23. Leonard MSS, J. H. Middleton and William Need, Indenture

to Fielding Lucas, Agent of Baltimore Type Foundry, May 4, 1833, Middleton and Need, Account with Baltimore Type Foundry, May 18, 1833 [actually June 1, 1836], J. F. Darby to A. Leonard, November 11, December 2, 1837, September 24, 1839, J. H. Middleton vs. Robert Brent, July 10, 1839 [actually November, 1839]; *Missouri Intelligencer* (Columbia), April 13, 1833, January 11, September 13, 20, December 27, 1834.

24. *The Western Emigrant* (Boonville), February 14, 1839.

25. *Missouri Gazette* (St. Louis), December 19, 1810; *The St. Louis Republic*, July 12, 1908.

26. *Missouri Argus* (St. Louis), October 25, 1838.

27. Dunklin Papers, C. Keemle to D. Dunklin, September 23, 1831.

28. *Missouri Intelligencer* (Columbia), December 27, 1834; *Jefferson Inquirer* (Jefferson City), December 24, 1840.

29. *Missouri Republican* (St. Louis), April 2, 1823, July 15, 1828; *Missouri Intelligencer* (Fayette), January 18, 1828, September 18, 1829; *The Weekly Tribune* (Liberty), August 7, 1847.

30. *Jefferson Inquirer* (Jefferson City), June 23, 1849.

31. *Missouri Gazette* (St. Louis), January 1, 1814; the quotation on the Indian is from *ibid.*, July 26, 1810.

32. Historical Records Survey, *A Preliminary Check List of Missouri Imprints, 1808–1850* (Washington, 1937), *passim*; J. M. Breckinridge, *William Clark Breckinridge* (St. Louis, 1932), pp. 253, 292.

33. *Missouri Gazette* (St. Louis), September 13, 1809. References to the mail situation are legion; the bound volumes of the newspapers contain many complaints of editors.

34. Postmaster R. J. Meigs to J. Charless, December 31, 1816, Carter, *Territorial Papers*, XV, p. 222.

35. W. E. Rich, *The History of the United States Post Office to the Year 1829* (Cambridge, 1924), pp. 98–99, 142–46.

36. *Ibid.*, pp. 144–46; United States Post Office Department, *Postage Rates 1798–1930* (Washington, 1930), pp. 2–5.

37. Missouri, *The Revised Statutes of the State of Missouri Revised and Digested by the Thirteenth General Assembly* (St. Louis: J. W. Dougherty, 1845), pp. 115–19.

38. *Missouri Gazette* (St. Louis), December 18, 1818.

39. *Missouri Intelligencer* (Columbia), January 15, 1831.

40. *Missouri Republican* (St. Louis), October 25, 1824. See also *Missouri Gazette* (St. Louis), December 7, 1808, November 30, May 23, 1811; *Missouri Intelligencer* (Franklin), December 10, 1819, and following, August 26, 1823, and *ibid.* (Fayette), September 21, 1826; *Missouri Argus* (St. Louis), June 12, 1835, October 25, 1838.

41. *Missouri Gazette* (St. Louis), March 9, 1816.

42. Auguste Chouteau Collection (Missouri Historical Society, St.

Louis), receipt to A. Chouteau from I. N. Henry and Co. by C. Keemle, June 23, 1819.

43. *Missouri Gazette* (St. Louis), January 11, 1812, March 29, 1817.

44. *Missouri Argus* (St. Louis), October 28, 1836.

45. Twain, *Autobiography*, II, p. 285.

46. *Missouri Intelligencer* (Columbia), December 22, 1832.

47. *Missouri Gazette* (St. Louis), November 23, 30, 1808, January 4, 1809; C. V. R. [Charles van Ravenswaay], "The Cover: Pioneer Presses in Missouri," *Bulletin of the Missouri Historical Society* (April, 1951), VII, p. 297.

48. *Missouri Intelligencer* (Fayette), May 16, 26, 1828.

49. *Ibid.* (Columbia), February 12, 1831.

50. Twain, *Autobiography*, II, 276–82.

51. *Jefferson Inquirer* (Jefferson City), July 11, 1835; *Missouri Intelligencer* (Columbia), July 11, 1835.

52. *Missouri Intelligencer* (Columbia), January 8, 15, 22, 1831; see also *ibid.* (Fayette), September 11, 1829.

53. *Missouri Gazette* (St. Louis), October 17, 1810.

54. *The Weekly Tribune* (Liberty), December 17, 1847.

CHAPTER 8

1. A. de Tocqueville, *Democracy in America* (New York, 1945), I, 186–87.

2. *Missouri Gazette* (St. Louis), July 19, 1817.

3. *Jefferson Inquirer* (Jefferson City), July 29, 1848.

4. *Jeffersonian Republican* (Jefferson City), December 20, 1834. Israel Putnam (1718–1790) is supposed to have killed a destructive wolf in its lair near his farm in Pomfret, Connecticut.

5. *Missouri Gazette* (St. Louis), July 19, 1817.

6. *Ibid.*, August 2, 1817.

7. W. N. Chambers, "Thomas Hart Benton: Editor," *Missouri Historical Review* (July, 1952), XLVI, 345.

8. *Missouri Argus* (St. Louis), April 14, 1837.

9. *Missouri Intelligencer* (Columbia), January 7, 1832.

10. *Ibid.*, September 27, 1834.

11. *Liberty Weekly Tribune*, November 18, 1853.

12. *Missouri Argus* (St. Louis), September 27, 1837. See also *Missouri Intelligencer* (Fayette), November 9, 1827.

13. *Missouri Gazette* (St. Louis), June 9, 23, November 3, 1819; on Joshua Norvell's refusal to print Joseph Charless' name in *Western Journal* see *ibid.*, August 5, 1815.

14. Reprints from *Boonville Herald, Western Monitor* (Fayette),

and *Salt River Journal* (Bowling Green), in *Missouri Intelligencer* (Columbia), February 22, 1834, June 6, July 4, 1835.

15. *Missouri Republican* (St. Louis), December 9, 23, 1828.

16. *Missouri Argus* (St. Louis), April 15, 1836.

17. *Ibid.*, June 19, 1835. For similar comments see also *ibid.*, April 22, 1836.

18. *Missouri Intelligencer* (Fayette), April 5, September 27, 1827, and *ibid.* (Columbia), December 3, 1831.

19. See, for instance, Patten in *St. Charles Clarion*, quoted in *Jeffersonian Republican* (Jefferson City), November 5, 1836.

20. *Missouri Argus* (St. Louis), April 14, 1837.

21. *Ibid.*, April 22, 1836.

22. *Ibid.*, October 9, 1835, February 26, March 18, 1836; *Missouri Register* (Boonville) August 9, 1843; *Missouri Intelligencer* (Columbia), January 12, 1833.

23. *Missouri Gazette* (St. Louis), November 12, 1814. For further comments by Charless see *ibid.*, January 21, August 5, November 19, 1815, September 13, 1820.

24. *Boonville Observer*, May 9, 1850.

25. *Missouri Intelligencer* (Columbia), April 30, 1831, February 16, July 11, May 2, 25, 1835.

26. U. S. Congress, *American State Papers, Documents, Legislative and Executive, of the Congress of the United States, Post Office Department* (Washington, 1834), Class vii, pp. 347–48.

27. *Missouri Intelligencer* (Columbia), February 16, 1833.

28. *Ibid.*, October 31, 1835.

29. *Ibid.*, October 31, November 14, 1835.

30. *Missouri Argus* (St. Louis), December 18, 1835.

31. Dunklin Papers (University of Missouri, Columbia), see D. Dunklin to Editor of St. Louis Argus [Corbin], September 26, 1835; Missouri, *Laws of the State of Missouri, 9th General Assembly, 1st Session* (City of Jefferson: Calvin Gunn, 1837), p. 317. His *Revised Statutes* were "Printed at the Argus Office": Missouri, *The Revised Statutes of the State of Missouri* (St. Louis: Printed at the Argus Office, 1835).

32. *Missouri Argus* (St. Louis), March 18, October 7, 1836; *Jefferson Inquirer* (Jefferson City), July 15, 29, 1848, March 30, 1850, April 30, 1853; *Liberty Weekly Tribune*, April 6, May 18, 1866, October 16, 1868; *The Daily Tribune* (Jefferson City), April 27, 1876.

33. *Missouri Intelligencer* (Fayette), February 27, 1829, March 19, 1830, and *ibid.* (Columbia), September 3, 10, 1831, December 22, 1832, August 9, 1834, May 2, November 21, 1835.

34. F. L. Billon, *Annals of St. Louis in its Territorial Days from 1804 to 1821* (St. Louis, 1888), pp. 314–15; *Missouri Republican* (St. Louis), November 7, 21, December 5, 1825, October 26, No-

vember 6, 1826, January 11, 1827, July 15, 1828; *Missouri Intelligencer* (Franklin), September 30, 1823, January 18, August 12, 1825; C. S. Brigham, *History and Bibliography of American Newspapers 1690–1820* (Worcester, 1947), I, 143; D. G. Brown, "Early St. Louis Newspapers, 1808–1850" (unpublished Master's thesis, Washington University, 1931), pp. 39–46, 70, 75–76, 81–84, 86–87; *Missouri Argus* (St. Louis), May 29, November 22, 1835, October 25, November 16, December 20, 1838 (many other references may be found in this paper to Keemle's social activities); Dunklin Papers, C. Keemle to D. Dunklin, September 23, 1831. Richard Edwards reported that Keemle refused to accept President Harrison's offer of appointment as Secretary of the Interior and President Taylor's appointment as Indian Agent. See R. Edwards and M. Hopewell, *Edwards's Great West* (St. Louis, 1860), p. 172.

35. *Missouri Gazette* (St. Louis), September 16, 1817, August 18, 1819; *Missouri Republican* (St. Louis), June 21, 1827.

36. *Missouri Gazette* (St. Louis), November 19, 1815, October 12, 1816, October 20, 1819; *Missouri Intelligencer* (Franklin), August 5, 1823, June 29, 1826; *Missouri Argus* (St. Louis), May 29, 1835; *Jefferson Inquirer* (St. Louis), October 10, 1844. James C. Cummins printed an extract from Laurence Sterne's *Tristram Shandy* in which Uncle Toby and Trim lamented the station of the poor printer who must try to please everybody and pleased nobody. *Missouri Gazette* (St. Louis), August 1, 1821.

37. *Missouri Intelligencer* (Columbia), June 23, 1832; see also *Independent Patriot* (Jackson), November 22, 1823.

38. *Jefferson Inquirer* (Jefferson City), December 24, 1840. The allusion to the coonskin is probably a reference to the symbol which flew over the office of the St. Louis *Missouri Republican*, a Whig paper.

39. See *Missouri Intelligencer* (Franklin), July 23, 1821, and *ibid.* (Columbia), March 23, 1833; *Independent Patriot* (Jackson), May 28, 1825; *Jefferson Inquirer*, (Jefferson City), October 24, 1844.

40. *Jeffersonian Republican* (Jefferson City), May 17, 1834.

41. *Missouri Intelligencer* (Columbia), July 4, 1835.

42. D. C. McMurtrie, *Joseph Charless, Pioneer Printer of St. Louis* (Chicago, 1931), p. 23.

43. *Missouri Gazette* (St. Louis), July 5, 1817.

44. *Missouri Argus* (St. Louis), April 14, 28, 1837.

45. *Ibid.*, August 29, 1839; *The Western Emigrant* (Boonville), September 5, 1839.

46. *Missouri Argus* (St. Louis), December 12, 1840.

47. *Boonville Observer*, February 17, March 31, 1846.

48. *Jefferson Inquirer* (Jefferson City), August 13, 1853.

49. *Boonville Observer*, April 29, 1854.

50. *Ibid.*, April 29, July 29, September 2, 1854; *Boonville Weekly Observer*, November 4, 1854.
51. *Liberty Weekly Tribune*, May 27, 1859.
52. *Ibid.*, June 24, 1859.

CHAPTER 9

1. *Missouri Intelligencer* (Fayette), February 6, 1829.
2. *Ibid.* (Columbia), December 5, 1835.
3. *Missouri Gazette* (St. Louis), September 8, 1819; *Missouri Intelligencer* (Columbia), March 23, 1833.
4. N. Webster, *A Dictionary of the English Language* (New York, 1830), p. 285.
5. *Missouri Intelligencer* (Franklin), August 5, 1825.
6. B. Fay, *Notes on the American Press at the End of the Eighteenth Century* (New York, 1927), p. 15. See also A. M. Schlesinger, *Prelude to Independence* (New York, 1958), *passim*.
7. J. W. Ridings, "Editorial Policies of the *Missouri Intelligencer*" (unpublished Master's thesis, University of Missouri, 1928), Plate I after p. 103.
8. M. Organ, "History of the County Press of Missouri," *Missouri Historical Review* (April, 1910), IV, p. 307.
9. *Missouri Gazette* (St. Louis), January 4, 1809.
10. See the various prospectuses for the editors' concept of what was newsworthy. Also Tubal E. Strange for the Jackson *Independent Patriot* in *St. Louis Enquirer*, May 5, 1819, and S. W. Foreman and R. M'Cloud for St. Charles *Missouri Gazette* in *Missouri Republican*, St. Louis, October 22, 1823.
11. *Missouri Intelligencer* (Fayette), June 29, 1826.
12. L. M. Salmon, *The Newspaper and the Historian* (New York, 1923), pp. 8–9, 152, 158–72.
13. *Missouri Gazette* (St. Louis), July 13, 1816.
14. L. L. Cooper, "A Study of Local News in the Missouri Weekly from 1831 to 1931" (unpublished Master's thesis, University of Missouri, 1932), pp. 26, 101–16.
15. *The Boonville Weekly Eagle*, June 23, 1876; *Jefferson City Daily Tribune*, February 21, 1894; *The St. Louis Republic*, July 12, 1908.
16. *Missouri Intelligencer* (Columbia), September 2, 1833.
17. F. W. Scott, *Newspapers and Periodicals of Illinois 1814–1879*, in *Collections of the Illinois State Historical Library* (Springfield, 1910), VI, xxxiii.
18. *Independent Patriot* (Jackson), January 6, 1821.
19. *Ibid.*, February 28, 1824.

20. *Missouri Republican* (St. Louis), September 6, 1824.

21. *Missouri Argus* (St. Louis), March 11, 1836.

22. *Jeffersonian Republican* (Jefferson City), January 11 to June 28, 1834. See also *Missouri Intelligencer* (Fayette), October 16, 1829, concerning the *Western Monitor* (Fayette); *Jefferson Inquirer* (Jefferson City), September 10, 1840; *St. Louis Enquirer*, December 30, 1818.

23. *Missouri Intelligencer* (Fayette), November 21, 1828, February 6, 1829.

24. *Missouri Intelligencer* (Franklin), June 16, 1826; *ibid.* (Fayette), Jnune 29, 1826; see also *Jefferson Inquirer* (Jefferson City), September 10, 1840.

25. *Jeffersonian Republican* (Jefferson City), March 26, 1836; *St. Louis Enquirer*, May 5, 1819.

26. *Missouri Intelligencer* (Fayette), September 11, 1829; *The Western Emigrant* (Boonville), February 14, 1839; *Boonville Observer*, April 14, 1846; *Independent Patriot* (Jackson), August 9, 1823.

27. Leonard MSS (State Historical Society of Missouri, Columbia), B. H. Reeves to A. Leonard, June 14, 1833.

28. *Missouri Intelligencer* (Fayette), January 1, 1830. See also *ibid.*, May 22, 1829; *Independent Patriot* (Jackson), November 6, 1824; *Liberty Weekly Tribune*, April 25, 1856.

29. C. B. Spotts, "The Development of Fiction on the Missouri Frontier (1830–1860)," *Missouri Historical Review* (July, 1934), XXVIII, 279; J. Viles, "Old Franklin: A Frontier Town of the Twenties," *Mississippi Valley Historical Review* (March, 1923), IX, 281–82.

30. *Jefferson Inquirer* (Jefferson City), June 23, 1849.

31. *Missouri Intelligencer* (Columbia), March 12, 1831, October 2, 1830.

32. *Missouri Gazette* (St. Louis), June 23, 1819.

33. *Missouri Republican* (St. Louis), July 1, 1828.

34. *Boonville Observer*, November 17, 1847; B. W. Elliott, "The Literary Editing of Nathaniel Patten, Jr., From 1822–1835 in *The Missouri Intelligencer*" (unpublished Master's thesis, University of Missouri, 1953), pp. 39–121; *Missouri Gazette* (St. Louis), September 13, 1820.

35. Spotts, "Fiction on Missouri Frontier," p. 297; Elliott, "Literary Editing of Patten," p. 64.

36. *Missouri Intelligencer* (Franklin), January 1, 1825. See in most newspapers the first issue after January 1 for the carriers' addresses.

37. H. O. Mahin, *The Development and Significance of the Newspaper Headline* (Ann Arbor, 1924), pp. vii–viii, 2–5, 24–25, 145; T. B. Hammond, "The Development of Journalism in Missouri, The

Newspaper" (unpublished Master's thesis, University of Missouri, 1922), p. 16.

38. See advertisement of type foundry in *Missouri Intelligencer* (Fayette), January 18, 1828, and *Missouri Republican* (St. Louis), January 17, 1828; *The Weekly Tribune* (Liberty), August 7, 1847.

39. A. de Tocqueville, *Democracy in America* (New York, 1945), I, 185.

40. A. B. Daspit, "The Evolution of Advertising in America as Exemplified in Missouri Newspapers " (unpublished Master's thesis, University of Missouri, 1930), pp. 6–15, 22–27; B. Z. Weinbach, "The Development of Advertising in Boone County, Missouri" (unpublished Master's thesis, University of Missouri, 1930), pp. 4–6, 18, 52; Hammond, "Development of Journalism," p. 52.

41. L. E. Atherton, *The Pioneer Merchant in Mid-America* (Columbia, Missouri, 1939), pp. 116–18, 124; *Jefferson Inquirer* (Jefferson City), August 13, 1853; *Boonville Observer*, February 17, March 31, 1846; *Missouri Intelligencer* (Columbia), December 22, 1832; *Missouri Gazette* (St. Louis), September 8, 1819.

42. Atherton, *Pioneer Merchant*, pp. 118–23.

43. Daspit, "Evolution of Advertising," p. 913; Weinbach, "Advertising in Boone County," pp. 24, 61.

44. Daspit, "Evolution of Advertising," pp. 16–18; Weinbach, "Advertising in Boone County," p. 24.

45. *Missouri Gazette* (St. Louis), April 11, 1811, April 19, 26, 1817; *Missouri Republican* (St. Louis), October 18, 1823; *Missouri Intelligencer* (Franklin), June 18, 1825.

46. *Boonville Observer*, June 24, 1846.

47. Daspit, "Evolution of Advertising," pp. 37–46; Atherton, *Pioneer Merchant*, pp. 123–24.

48. *Missouri Gazette*, December 14, 1816; *Liberty Weekly Tribune*, November 8, 1850.

49. Atherton, *Pioneer Merchant*, pp. 123–24; Daspit, "Evolution of Advertising," p. 43.

CHAPTER 10

1. B. Fay, *Notes on the American Press at the End of the Eighteenth Century* (New York, 1927), Facsimile I (italics omitted).

2. United States Post Office Department, *Postage Rates 1789–1930* (Washington, 1930), p. 6.

3. W. E. Rich, *The History of the United States Post Office to the Year 1829* (Cambridge, 1924), pp. 80, 87, 99–100, 142–43. That the editor often was left without anything to print because of the failure of the mail has been discussed. See pp. 142–43, and also *Missouri Gazette* (St. Louis), February 28, 1811; *Missouri Intelli-*

gencer (Franklin), February 21, March 13, 1824, and *ibid.* (Columbia), November 23, 1833, January 25, 1834; Sergeant Hall to Secretary of State [Adams], March 29, 1818, in C. E. Carter, comp. and ed., *The Territorial Papers of the United States, The Territory of Louisiana-Missouri, 1815–1821* (Washington, 1951), XV, 368–69.

4. *Missouri Gazette* (St. Louis), January 21, 1815; see also *Missouri Intelligencer* (Fayette), October 9, 1829, for James H. Birch of the *Western Monitor* refusing to give up an author, and Leonard MSS (State Historical Society of Missouri, Columbia) B. H. Reeves to A. Leonard, July 30, 1832, for a similar refusal of B. Emmons Ferry, also of the *Western Monitor.*

5. *Missouri Intelligencer* (Columbia), July 13, 1833.

6. *Missouri Gazette* (St. Louis), October 31, 1810, January 21, 1815; *Missouri Intelligencer* (Franklin), July 23, 1821, November 11, 1825; *Jefferson Inquirer* (Jefferson City), January 27, 1842, January 12, 1843; *Independent Patriot* (Jackson), July 21, 1821; *Missouri Argus* (St. Louis), May 29, 1835.

7. *Missouri Republican* (St. Louis), November 7, 21, December 5, 1825. Benton killed the younger Lucas in a duel in 1817. In the first encounter between the two, Benton wounded his opponent, but Benton demanded that one or the other be killed and in the second encounter, Benton did kill him. Also, the elder Lucas opposed Benton in the first senatorial election.

8. *Ibid.*, March 30, 1826.

9. *The Weekly Tribune* (Liberty), October 8, 1847.

10. Sibley Papers (Missouri Historical Society, St. Louis), A. B. Chambers to G. C. Sibley, September 25, 1839.

11. Dunklin Papers (University of Missouri, Columbia), F. H. Martin to D. Dunklin, September [?], 1835, D. Dunklin to F. H. Martin, September 26, 1835; *Missouri Argus* (St. Louis), September 11, 14, 1835.

12. Dunklin Papers, F. H. Martin to D. Dunklin, July 24, 1835.

13. *Missouri Gazette* (St. Louis), May 12, 1819.

14. *Missouri Intelligencer* (Columbia), February 23, 1833.

15. *Missouri Republican* (St. Louis), March 20, 1822.

16. See p. 79.

17. Missouri, *Journal of the House, 8th General Assembly* (Fayette: W. B. Napton, 1835), p. 6; E. E. Sparlin, "The *Jefferson Inquirer*" (unpublished Master's thesis, University of Missouri, 1932), pp. 33–34.

18. Leonard MSS, B. H. Reeves to A. Leonard, January 1, 1835; *Missouri Intelligencer* (Columbia), January 10, 1835.

19. *St. Louis Enquirer*, December 23, 1818; Leonard MSS, A. S. Mitchell to A. Leonard, September 3, 1852, J. O. Broadhead to A. Leonard, March 16, 1851.

20. *Jefferson Inquirer* (Jefferson City), October 24, 1844.

21. *Boonville Observer*, January 6, 1846.

22. *Missouri Gazette* (St. Louis), August 1, 1821.

23. L. L. Cooper, "A Study of Local News in the Missouri Weekly from 1831 to 1931" (unpublished Master's thesis, University of Missouri, 1932), p. 14; B. E. Birkhead, " A Study of the *Missouri Gazette* through the Editorship of its Founder, Joseph Charless" (unpublished Master's thesis, University of Missouri, 1945), pp. 62–63.

24. *Jeffersonian Republican* (Jefferson City), March 15, 1834.

25. *Missouri Gazette* (St. Louis), November 30, December 7, 1808, March 22, 1809.

26. *Jefferson Inquirer* (Jefferson City), October 29, November 26, 1840.

27. *Boonville Observer*, March 17, 1846; see also *Missouri Republican* (St. Louis), May 17, 1827.

28. *Missouri Gazette* (St. Louis), June 27, August 8, 1811.

29. *Ibid.*, January 13, February 13, 1816.

30. *Liberty Weekly Tribune*, January 30, 1852.

31. See for instance *St. Louis Enquirer*, November 20, 1819; *The Western Emigrant* (Boonville), January 24, 1839; *Boonville Observer*, April 28, 1846.

32. *Missouri Gazette* (St. Louis), July 13, 1816.

33. *Missouri Intelligencer* (Columbia), August 29, 1835.

34. Leonard MSS, A. S. Mitchell to A. Leonard, May 26, 1852.

EPILOGUE

1. A. de Tocqueville, *Democracy in America* (New York, 1945), I, 325.

2. *Missouri Argus* (St. Louis), March 24, 1837.

INDEX

191